*quick and easy tastes of*
# thailand

Styling  DONNA HAY
Photography  WILLIAM MEPPEM

**TRIDENT PRESS**
INTERNATIONAL

# Introduction

*Fresh coriander, chillies, garlic, coconut, fish sauce and citrus flavourings are the six ingredients that identify Thai cooking. These foods combine to create a style of food which has the subtle complex flavours generally associated with Oriental cuisines, but is clean, vivid and very definitely Thai. It is a cuisine that is meant to be enjoyed by all – including the cook – and as such, all the dishes are placed on the table at the one time and as long as the rice is steaming hot, it really doesn't matter if the other dishes are not.*

*Rather than following completely authentic Thai recipes, the ones in this book are based on traditional recipes and cooking techniques which reflect a style and type of cuisine that will appeal to the modern cook*

Published by:
TRIDENT PRESS INTERNATIONAL
801 12th Avenue South
Suite 302
Naples, FL 34102 U.S.A.
(c)Trident Press
Tel: (941) 649 7077
Fax: (941) 649 5832
Email: tridentpress@worldnet.att.net
Website: www.trident-international.com

Quick & Easy Tastes of Thailand

Managing Editor: Rachel Blackmore
Editorial and Production Assistant: Heather Straton
Editorial Coordinator: Margaret Kelly

Photography: William Meppem
Styling and Food: Donna Hay
Food Stylist's Assistant and
Recipe Development: Angela Nahas

DESIGN AND PRODUCTION
Production Director: Anna Maguire
Design Manager: Drew Buckmaster
Production Coordination: Meredith Johnston
Production Coordinator: Sophie Potter
Layout and Design: Lulu Dougherty
Production Editor: Sheridan Packer

Includes Index
ISBN 1 58279 343 3
EAN 9 781582 793436

First Edition Printed August 2001

Printed by Toppan Printing, China

## COOKING NOTES

**Basil:** In this book the type of basil is not specified. Ordinary sweet basil can be used however the Thai cook would use Asian sweet, holy or lemon basil depending on the dish – for more information see Glossary on page 78.

**Canned foods:** Can sizes vary between countries and manufacturers. You may find the quantities in this book are slightly different to what is available. Purchase and use the can size nearest to the suggested size in the recipe.

**Cream:** Unless otherwise stated the cream used in this book is double – suitable for whipping.

**Flour:** The flour used in this book is white, plain or standard flour – if another type of flour has been used it is stated.

**Rice:** For an authentic Thai meal serve piping hot steamed jasmine rice – it should be cooked without salt. In Thailand rice is the central dish of any meal and the other dishes are considered to be side dishes.

**Serving sizes:** In this book the serving sizes have been calculated with the Western way of eating in mind. If you are serving a meal in the Thai style then the recipes will serve at least 2-4 more than stated.

**Shallots:** The shallots used in this book are a small golden, purple or red onion. They are 2.5-5 cm/1-2 in long and have a more intense flavour than large onions. The golden shallots are sweeter than the red or purple ones – for more information see Glossary on page 80.

**Sugar:** Unless otherwise stated the sugar used in this book is white.

Additional information about ingredients used in this book can be found in the Glossary on page 78.

What's in a Tablespoon?

AUSTRALIA
1 tablespoon = 20 mL or 4 teaspoons
NEW ZEALAND
1 tablespoon = 15 mL or 3 teaspoons
UNITED KINGDOM
1 tablespoon = 15 mL or 3 teaspoons

The recipes in this book were tested in Australia where a 20 mL tablespoon is standard. The tablespoon in the New Zealand and the United Kingdom sets of measuring spoons is 15 mL. For recipes using baking powder, gelatine, bicarbonate of soda, small quantities of flour and cornflour, simply add another teaspoon for each tablespoon specified.

# Contents

6
Snacks & Starters

16
Soups

22
Salads

30
Stir-fries

42
Curries

54
Steamed, Grilled
& Fried

76
Easy Thai Dinner
for Six

78
Glossary

64
Rice & Noodles

70
Sweets

81
Index

# SNACKS & STARTERS

# CHICKEN SATAY

500 g/1 lb boneless chicken breast
fillets, cut into 1 cm/$^1$/2 in wide strips
2 cloves garlic, crushed
1 tablespoon finely grated fresh ginger
1 teaspoon ground coriander
3 tablespoons light soy sauce

SATAY SAUCE
6 red shallots or 1 small red onion
2 fresh red chillies, roughly chopped
1 clove garlic, crushed
$^1$/2 teaspoon shrimp paste (optional)
1 tablespoon vegetable oil
$^1$/2 cup/125 mL/4 fl oz coconut milk
2 tablespoons light soy sauce
1 tablespoon lime juice
90 g/3 oz roasted chopped peanuts

1   Thread chicken onto lightly oiled
bamboo skewers and place in a shallow
glass or ceramic dish. Combine garlic,
ginger, coriander and soy sauce and
pour over skewers. Cover and marinate
in the refrigerator for 30 minutes.

2   To make sauce, place shallots or
onion, chillies, garlic and shrimp paste
(if using) in a food processor or blender
and process to make a smooth paste.
Heat oil in a wok or frying pan over a
high heat, add paste and cook, stirring,
for 3 minutes or until golden. Stir in
coconut milk, soy sauce, lime juice and
peanuts and cook, stirring, until mixture
is heated through. If the sauce is too
thick add a little water.

3   Drain skewers and cook under a
preheated hot grill or on a hot barbecue
grill for 2 minutes each side or until
cooked. Serve with sauce.

**Beef Satay:** Use 500 g/1 lb lean topside
or round steak in place of the chicken.
**Pork Satay:** Use 500 g/1 lb lean pork
fillets or steak in place of the chicken.

*Makes 12*

A small food processor or a held-hand blender is ideal for making curry pastes. The ordinary domestic food processor is often too large for the small quantities of ingredients used. Alternatively, pastes can be made using a mortar and pestle – this is the traditional method of preparation in Thailand.

# HERBED VEGETABLE ROLLS

12 large Oriental rice paper rounds
sweet chilli sauce

HERBED VEGETABLE FILLING
2 cucumbers, seeded and cut into
5 cm/2 in strips
2 carrots, cut into 5 cm/2 in strips
60 g/2 oz bean sprouts
60 g/2 oz rice vermicelli noodles,
cooked and drained well
30 g/1 oz fresh mint leaves
30 g/1 oz fresh basil leaves
15 g/$^1$/2 oz fresh coriander leaves
4 tablespoons chopped roasted peanuts
12 garlic chives with flower (optional)

1   Dip a rice paper round into cold
water, then place on a clean teatowel,
to absorb any excess moisture.

2   To assemble, place a little of the
cucumber, carrot, sprouts, noodles,
mint, basil, coriander and peanuts
along the centre of each rice paper
round leaving a 2 cm/$^3$/4 in border.
Place a chive (if using) across the
centre so that the end with the flower
hangs over one edge.

3   To roll, fold up one edge of rice
paper over filling to form base of roll,
then roll up to enclose filling. Repeat
with remaining rice paper rounds,
filling and chives. Serve immediately
with chilli sauce for dipping.

*Makes 12*

Traditionally the garlic chive pops out the open end of the roll as a garnish. Oriental rice paper is made from a paste of ground rice and water which is stamped into rounds and dried. When moistened the brittle sheets become flexible. It is used to make delicacies such as these rolls. Sold in sealed packets rice paper can be purchased from Oriental food stores.

# CRISPY NOODLES WITH LIME PICKLE

220 g/7 oz cellophane noodles
6 small fresh red chillies, finely sliced
4 red or golden shallots, finely chopped
30 g/1 oz fresh coriander leaves,
chopped
30 g/1 oz fresh basil leaves, chopped
1 tablespoon roasted shrimp paste
(optional)
$^{1}/_{4}$ cup/60 mL/2 fl oz peanut oil

LIME PICKLE
4 limes, sliced
6 red or golden shallots, sliced
1 tablespoon salt
$^{1}/_{2}$ cup/125 mL/4 fl oz water
$^{1}/_{2}$ cup/90 g/3 oz brown sugar
$^{1}/_{4}$ cup/60 mL/2 fl oz vinegar
1 tablespoon Thai fish sauce (nam pla)
1 tablespoon black mustard seeds

1  To make pickle, place limes, shallots, salt and water in a saucepan and cook, stirring occasionlly, over a medium heat for 10-15 minutes or until limes are tender. Stir in sugar, vinegar, fish sauce and mustard seeds and simmer, stirring frequently, for 30 minutes or until pickle is thick. Serve immediately or pour into a sterilised jar, seal and store in the refrigerator.

2  Place noodles in a bowl, pour over boiling water to cover and stand for 10 minutes or until soft. Drain well. Add chillies, shallots, coriander, basil and shrimp paste (if using) to noodles and mix well.

3  Heat oil in a large frying pan over a medium heat, place small handfuls of noodle mixture in pan, shape into a rough round and flatten with a spatula. Cook for 3-4 minutes each side or until golden and crisp. Drain on absorbent kitchen paper and serve with pickle.

*Serves 6*

When making the pickle take care not to let it catch on the bottom of the pan. The pickle can be made in advance and stored in the refrigerator or if keeping for more than 2 weeks seal in a sterilised jar.

*Crispy Noodles with Lime Pickle*

# STEAMED CRAB AND PORK BALLS

**12 English spinach leaves**

CRAB AND PORK FILLING
**315 g/10 oz pork mince**
**185 g/6 oz canned crab meat, drained**
**1 stalk fresh lemon grass, finely chopped, or $^1/_2$ teaspoon dried lemon grass, soaked in hot water until soft**
**1 tablespoon shredded fresh or bottled galangal or fresh ginger**
**3 tablespoons chopped fresh coriander leaves and stems**
**4 kaffir lime leaves, finely shredded**
**1 clove garlic, crushed**
**1 tablespoon ground coriander**
**1 tablespoon ground cumin**
**1 egg white, lightly beaten**
**1 tablespoon Thai fish sauce (nam pla)**

SWEET CHILLI SAUCE
**1 cup/170 g/5$^1/_2$ oz palm or brown sugar**
**1 stalk fresh lemon grass, bruised, or $^1/_2$ teaspoon dried lemon grass, soaked in hot water until soft**
**5 cm/2 in piece fresh galangal or ginger, cut in half, or 6 slices bottled galangal**
**4 small fresh red chillies, finely sliced**
**$^1/_2$ cup/125 mL/4 fl oz water**
**finely grated rind and juice of 2 limes**
**2 tablespoons Thai fish sauce (nam pla)**

1  To make filling, place pork, crab meat, lemon grass, galangal or ginger, fresh coriander, lime leaves, garlic, ground coriander, cumin, egg white and fish sauce in a food processor and process until smooth.

2  Steam or microwave spinach leaves until they are just soft. Roll 2 tablespoons of filling into a ball and place in the centre of each spinach leaf. Fold leaf around filling to enclose.

3  Half fill a clean wok with hot water and bring to the boil. Place balls in a bamboo steamer lined with nonstick baking paper. Cover steamer, place on a wire rack in wok and steam for 10-12 minutes or until cooked through.

4  To make sauce, place sugar, lemon grass, galangal or ginger, chillies, water, lime rind and juice and fish sauce in a saucepan and cook, stirring, over a medium heat for 10 minutes or until sauce reduces slightly. Remove lemon grass and galangal or ginger and discard. Serve sauce with rolls.

*Makes 12*

Galangal belongs to the same family as ginger. In Thai cooking it is usually greater galangal that is used and where other Asian cuisines would use ginger, the Thais use galangal. It can be purchased fresh or bottled in brine. Bottled galangal is more tender and not as fibrous as the fresh product and as such is somewhat easier to use. Bottled galangal will keep for months in the refrigerator. If unavailable fresh ginger can be used, but the finished dish will have a different flavour.

*Steamed Crab and Pork Balls,*
*Rice Cakes with Lime Crab*

# RICE CAKES WITH LIME CRAB

2 cups/440 g/14 oz jasmine rice, cooked
30 g/1 oz fresh coriander leaves,
chopped
crushed black peppercorns
vegetable oil for deep-frying

LIME CRAB TOPPING
185 g/6 oz canned crab meat,
well-drained
2 fresh red chillies, seeded and chopped
2 small fresh green chillies, finely sliced
$^1$/4 cup/60 mL/2 fl oz coconut cream
2 tablespoons thick natural yogurt
3 teaspoons lime juice
3 teaspoons Thai fish sauce (nam pla)
3 teaspoons finely grated lime rind
1 tablespoon crushed black peppercorns

*Makes 24*

1  Combine rice, coriander and black peppercorns to taste, then press into an oiled 18 x 28 cm/7 x 11 in shallow cake tin and refrigerate until set. Cut rice mixture into 3 x 4 cm/1$^1$/4 x 1$^1$/2 in rectangles.

2  Heat vegetable oil in a large saucepan until a cube of bread dropped in browns in 50 seconds and cook rice cakes, a few at a time, for 3 minutes or until golden. Drain on absorbent kitchen paper.

3  To make topping, place crab meat, red and green chillies, coconut cream, yogurt, lime juice and fish sauce in a food processor and process until smooth. Stir in lime rind and black peppercorns. Serve with warm rice cakes.

Coconut milk and coconut cream are essentially the same product. Coconut cream is very thick coconut milk and is the result of the first pressing of the coconut flesh. Coconut milk and cream can be purchased in various forms or you can make them yourself – for more information see Glossary on page 78.

# MUSSELS WITH TAMARIND

1 kg/2 lb mussels, scrubbed and
beards removed
2 stalks fresh lemon grass, bruised, or
1 teaspoon dried lemon grass, soaked
in hot water until soft
8 kaffir lime leaves, torn into pieces
5 cm/2 in piece fresh ginger, sliced
3 fresh coriander plants, roots
chopped, leaves chopped and reserved
$^1/_2$ cup/125 mL/4 fl oz water
$^1/_2$ cup/30 g/1 oz breadcrumbs, made
from stale bread

## TAMARIND AND CHILLI DRESSING
1-2 small dried red chillies, finely
chopped
2 teaspoons sugar
2 teaspoons finely grated lime rind
2 teaspoons shrimp paste (optional)
2 tablespoons tamarind concentrate
1 tablespoon Thai fish sauce (nam pla)

Shrimp paste is a pungent ingredient available from Oriental food shops and some supermarkets. It is made by pounding dried salted shrimp to a paste. Do not be put off by the odour as this disappears when the paste is cooked with other ingredients.

1  Place mussels, lemon grass, lime leaves, ginger, coriander roots and water in a saucepan, cover and bring to the boil. Reduce heat and simmer for 4-5 minutes or until mussels open. Remove from heat and discard any mussels that have not opened after 5 minutes cooking.

2  Strain mussels and reserve 2 tablespoons of the cooking liquid. Remove mussel meat from shells and place back in one half shell. Place mussels on a baking tray and discard remaining half shells.

3  To make dressing, place chillies, sugar, lime rind, shrimp paste (if using), tamarind concentrate, fish sauce and reserved cooking liquid in a bowl and whisk to combine.

4  Drizzle a little dressing over mussels. Combine breadcrumbs and reserved coriander leaves, sprinkle over mussels and cook under a preheated hot grill for 1-2 minutes or until topping is golden. Serve with remaining dressing.

*Serves 6*

*Mussels with Tamarind*

# FISH CAKES WITH RELISH

500 g/1 lb boneless fine fleshed
fish fillets
3 tablespoons Thai red curry paste
2 tablespoons chopped fresh coriander
leaves
1 tablespoon fresh basil leaves
1 egg white
90 g/3 oz green beans, finely chopped
2 kaffir lime leaves, finely shredded
(optional)
vegetable oil for shallow-frying

CUCUMBER RELISH
1 cucumber, seeded and chopped
1 fresh red chilli, chopped
1 tablespoon sugar
2 tablespoons rice vinegar
1 tablespoon water
1 tablespoon chopped roasted peanuts
(optional)

1   Place fish, curry paste, coriander,
basil and egg white in a food processor
and process to make a smooth thick
paste. Place mixture in a bowl, add
beans and lime leaves (if using) and
mix to combine. Cover and refrigerate
for 1 hour.

2   To make relish, place cucumber,
chilli, sugar, vinegar, water and peanuts
(if using) in a bowl and mix to
combine. Cover and refrigerate until
required.

3   Using wet or lightly oiled hands,
take 2 tablespoons of fish mixture and
roll into a ball, then flatten to form a
disk. Repeat with remaining fish mixture.

4   Heat about 2.5 cm/1 in oil in a
frying pan over a high heat and cook
fish cakes, a few at a time, for 2 minutes
each side or until well browned and
cooked through. Drain on absorbent
kitchen paper and serve hot fish cakes
with relish.

*Makes 12-14*

Rice vinegar is made from
fermented rice and
generally it is milder than
Western vinegars.
If unavailable, diluted white
or cider vinegar can be
used instead.

*Fish Cakes with Relish*

13

# PORK SPRING ROLLS

24 spring roll wrappers, each
12.5 cm/5 in square
vegetable oil for deep-frying
sweet chilli sauce

PORK AND CORIANDER FILLING
2 teaspoons peanut oil
3 red or golden shallots, chopped
2 teaspoons finely grated fresh ginger
1 fresh red chilli, seeded and chopped
500 g/1 lb pork mince
2 tablespoons chopped fresh coriander
leaves
2 tablespoons kechap manis

1   To make filling, heat peanut oil in a
frying pan over a high heat, add shallots,
ginger and chilli and stir-fry for
2 minutes. Add pork and stir-fry for
4-5 minutes or until pork is brown. Stir
in coriander and kechap manis and

cook for 2 minutes longer. Remove pan
from heat and set aside to cool.

2   To assemble, place 2 tablespoons of
filling in the centre of each wrapper,
fold one corner over filling, then tuck
in sides, roll up and seal with a little
water.

3   Heat vegetable oil in a wok or large
saucepan until a cube of bread dropped
in browns in 50 seconds and cook spring
rolls, a few at a time, for 3-4 minutes
or until crisp and golden. Drain on
absorbent kitchen paper and serve with
chilli sauce for dipping.

*Makes 24*

When working with spring
roll and wonton wrappers
place them under a damp
teatowel to prevent them
from drying out.
Kechap manis is a thick
sweet seasoning sauce. It is
made from soy sauce, sugar
and spices. If unavailable
soy sauce or a mixture of soy
sauce and dark corn syrup
can be used in its place.

# BEEF CURRY PUFFS

625 g/1¼ lb prepared puff pastry
vegetable oil for deep-frying
sweet chilli sauce

SPICY BEEF FILLING
2 teaspoons vegetable oil
4 red or golden shallots, chopped
1 tablespoon mild curry paste
2 teaspoons ground cumin
500 g/1 lb beef mince
2 tablespoons chopped fresh
coriander leaves

1   To make filling, heat oil in a frying
pan over a high heat, add shallots, curry
paste and cumin and stir-fry for
2 minutes. Add beef and stir-fry for
5 minutes or until brown. Remove pan
from heat and stir in coriander. Set
aside to cool.

2   Roll out pastry to 3 mm/⅛ in thick
and cut into 10 cm/4 in squares. With
one point of the pastry square facing you,
place 2-3 tablespoons of filling in the
centre and lightly brush edges with
water, then fold over point to meet the
one opposite. Press together and roll
edges to form a crescent-shaped parcel.
Repeat with remaining pastry and filling.

3   Heat vegetable oil in a large saucepan
until a cube of bread dropped in browns
in 50 seconds and cook puffs, a few at
a time, for 2 minutes or until puffed
and golden. Drain on absorbent
kitchen paper and serve with chilli
sauce for dipping.

*Makes 24*

Rather than deep-frying, the
curry puffs can be baked in
the oven. Simply place puffs
on lightly greased baking
trays, brush with a little milk
and bake at 220°C/425°F/
Gas 7 for 10-15 minutes or
until pastry is puffed and
golden.

*Beef Curry Puffs, Pork Spring Rolls*

# SOUPS

# HOT AND SOUR PRAWN SOUP

*Previous pages: Hot and Sour Prawn Soup, Chicken and Coconut Soup*

1 kg/2 lb medium uncooked prawns
1 tablespoon vegetable oil
8 slices fresh or bottled galangal or
fresh ginger
8 kaffir lime leaves
2 stalks fresh lemon grass, bruised, or
1 teaspoon dried lemon grass, soaked
in hot water until soft
2 fresh red chillies, halved and seeded
8 cups/2 litres/3$^1$/$_2$ pt water
3 tablespoons fresh coriander leaves
1 fresh red chilli, chopped
2 tablespoons lime juice
shredded kaffir lime leaves

1   Shell prawns and devein. Reserve heads and shells. Heat oil in a large saucepan over a high heat, add prawn heads and shells and cook, stirring, for 5 minutes or until shells change colour. Stir in galangal or ginger, lime leaves, lemon grass, halved chillies and water, cover and bring to simmering. Simmer, stirring occasionally, for 15 minutes.

2   Strain liquid into a clean saucepan and discard solids. Add prawns and cook for 2 minutes. Stir in coriander, chopped chilli and lime juice and cook for 1 minute or until prawns are tender. Ladle soup into bowls and garnish with shredded lime leaves.

*Serves 4*

This is the popular Thai soup known as Tom Yum Goong. Soups are an important dish and are served at almost every Thai meal, including breakfast which often starts with a bland rice soup.

# CHICKEN AND COCONUT SOUP

3 cups/750 mL/1$^1$/$_4$ pt coconut milk
2 cups/500 mL/16 fl oz water
500 g/1 lb chicken breast fillets, cut
into 1 cm/$^1$/$_2$ in thick strips
4 cm/1$^1$/$_2$ in piece fresh galangal or
ginger, sliced, or 6 slices bottled
galangal
2 stalks fresh lemon grass, cut into
4 cm/1$^1$/$_2$ in pieces, or 1 teaspoon
dried lemon grass, soaked in hot water
until soft
1 fresh coriander root, bruised
4 kaffir lime leaves, shredded
3 fresh red chillies, seeded and chopped
2 tablespoons Thai fish sauce (nam pla)
2 tablespoons lemon juice
fresh coriander leaves

1   Place coconut milk and water in a saucepan and bring to the boil over a medium heat, add chicken, galangal or ginger, lemon grass, coriander root and lime leaves and simmer for 6 minutes.

2   Stir in chillies, fish sauce and lemon juice. To serve, ladle into bowls and scatter with coriander leaves.

*Serves 6*

This popular Thai soup is known as Tom Kha Gai. When dining in the traditional Thai manner soups are not served as a separate course but are eaten with the other dishes and rice.

# HOT AND SOUR SEAFOOD SOUP

*Hot and Sour Seafood Soup*

4 red or golden shallots, sliced
2 fresh green chillies, chopped
6 kaffir lime leaves
4 slices fresh ginger
8 cups/2 litres/3$^1$/2 pt fish, chicken
or vegetable stock
250 g/8 oz boneless firm fish fillets,
cut into chunks
12 medium uncooked prawns, shelled
and deveined
12 mussels, scrubbed and beards
removed
125 g /4 oz oyster or straw mushrooms
3 tablespoons lime juice
2 tablespoons Thai fish sauce (nam pla)
fresh coriander leaves
lime wedges

1   Place shallots, chillies, lime leaves, ginger and stock in a saucepan and bring to the boil over a high heat. Reduce heat and simmer for 3 minutes.

2   Add fish, prawns, mussels and mushrooms and cook for 3-5 minutes or until fish and seafood are cooked, discard any mussels that do not open after 5 minutes cooking. Stir in lime juice and fish sauce. To serve, ladle soup into bowls, scatter with coriander leaves and accompany with lime wedges.

*Serves 6*

Straw mushrooms are one of the most popular mushrooms used in Asian cooking and in the West are readily available canned. Oyster mushrooms are also known as abalone mushrooms and range in colour from white to grey to pale pink. Their shape is similar to that of an oyster shell and they have a delicate flavour. Oyster mushrooms should not be eaten raw as some people are allergic to them in the uncooked state.

# THAI VEGETABLE SOUP

1 tablespoon chilli oil
4 red or golden shallots, chopped
3 stalks fresh lemon grass, cut into
pieces, or 1¹/₂ teaspoons dried lemon
grass, soaked in hot water until soft
4 slices fresh or bottled galangal or
fresh ginger
8 cups/2 litres/3¹/₂ pt vegetable stock
250 g/8 oz firm tofu, cubed
125 g/4 oz oyster mushrooms
125 g/4 oz snake (yard-long) or
green beans, chopped
30 g/1 oz bean sprouts
1 cup/250 mL/8 fl oz coconut milk
2 tablespoons fresh basil leaves
3 tablespoons finely chopped peanuts

1  Heat oil in a saucepan over a high heat, add shallots and lemon grass and cook, stirring, for 3 minutes. Stir in galangal or ginger and stock, then reduce heat and simmer for 5 minutes.

2  Add tofu, mushrooms, beans, bean sprouts and coconut milk and cook over a medium heat for 4 minutes or until beans are tender and soup is heated. To serve, ladle into bowls and scatter with basil and peanuts.

*Serves 6*

Snake (yard-long) beans, as their name suggests, are very long thin green beans. They are known by a variety names including asparagus bean, pea bean, cow pea and China pea. It is the dried seeds of this bean which become black-eyed peas.

# CHILLI KUMARA SOUP

6 cups/1.5 litres/2¹/₂ pt chicken stock
3 stalks fresh lemon grass, bruised, or
1¹/₂ teaspoons dried lemon grass,
soaked in hot water until soft
3 fresh red chillies, halved
10 slices fresh or bottled galangal or
fresh ginger
5-6 fresh coriander plants, roots
washed, leaves removed and reserved
1 large kumara (orange sweet potato),
peeled and cut into 2 cm/³/₄ in pieces
³/₄ cup/185 mL/6 fl oz coconut cream
1 tablespoon Thai fish sauce (nam pla)

2  Remove lemon grass, galangal or ginger and coriander roots and discard. Cool liquid slightly, then purée soup, in batches, in a food processor or blender. Return soup to a clean saucepan and stir in ¹/₂ cup/125 mL/4 fl oz of the coconut cream and the fish sauce. Cook, stirring, over a medium heat for 4 minutes or until heated. Stir in two-thirds of the reserved coriander leaves.

3  To serve, ladle soup into bowls, top with a little of the remaining coconut cream and scatter with remaining coriander leaves.

*Serves 4*

Coriander is used extensively in Thai cooking and it is one of the ingredients that gives Thai food its distinctive flavour. Fresh coriander is readily available from greengrocers and is usually sold as the whole plant.

1  Place stock, lemon grass, chillies, galangal or ginger and coriander roots in a saucepan and bring to the boil over a medium heat. Add kumara (sweet potato) and simmer, uncovered, for 15 minutes or until kumara (sweet potato) is soft.

*Thai Vegetable Soup,*
*Chilli Kumara Soup*

# SALADS

# CHICKEN SALAD WITH BASIL

In Thailand, salads are often assembled from the leaves of the many uncultivated shrubs and trees which grow along the roadsides, riverbanks and canals. This makes it somewhat difficult to reproduce an authentic Thai salad outside of Thailand. However the Western cook should be prepared to experiment with different vegetables and herbs to make interesting and tasty combinations.

2 teaspoons vegetable oil
4 chicken breast fillets
125 g/4 oz assorted lettuce leaves
30 g/1 oz fresh mint leaves
30 g/1 oz fresh basil leaves

CHILLI AND BASIL DRESSING
2 tablespoons sugar
2 tablespoons shredded fresh basil
1 fresh red chilli, sliced
3 tablespoons lime juice
2 tablespoons light soy sauce
2 teaspoons Thai fish sauce (nam pla)

1  Heat oil in a wok or frying pan over a high heat, add chicken and cook for 2-3 minutes each side or until just cooked through. Set aside to cool, then cut into thin slices.

2  Arrange lettuce, mint and basil leaves attractively on a serving platter, then top with chicken.

3  To make dressing, place sugar, shredded basil, chilli, lime juice and soy and fish sauces in a bowl and mix to combine. Drizzle dressing over salad and serve immediately.

*Serves 4*

# GREEN MANGO SALAD

Palm sugar is a rich, aromatic sugar extracted from the sap of various palms. The palm sugar used in Thailand is lighter and more refined than that used in other parts of Asia. Palm sugar is available from Oriental food shops.
If green (unripe) mangoes are unavailable you might like to make this salad using tart green apples instead.

125 g/4 oz mixed lettuce leaves
1 cucumber, thinly sliced
2 green (unripe) mangoes, peeled and thinly sliced
250 g/8 oz cooked chicken, shredded
4 tablespoons fresh mint leaves
4 tablespoons fresh coriander leaves

CHILLI AND LIME DRESSING
2 fresh red chillies, chopped
2 tablespoons palm or brown sugar
3 tablespoons lime juice
2 teaspoons Thai fish sauce (nam pla)

1  Arrange lettuce, cucumber, mangoes, chicken, mint and coriander attractively on a serving platter.

2  To make dressing, place chillies, sugar, lime juice and fish sauce in a bowl and mix to combine. Drizzle dressing over salad and serve.

*Serves 4*

*Rose Petal Salad*

# ROSE PETAL SALAD

2 tablespoons vegetable oil
2 onions, sliced
4 cloves garlic, sliced
8 lettuce leaves
4 red or golden shallots, chopped
250 g/8 oz pork fillets, cooked
and sliced
185 g/6 oz cooked prawns, shelled
and deveined
1 chicken breast fillet, cooked
and sliced
30 g/1 oz chopped roasted peanuts
20-30 fragrant rose petals, washed

LIME DRESSING
1 tablespoon sugar
4 tablespoons Thai fish sauce (nam pla)
4 tablespoons lime juice

1   Heat oil in a frying pan over a medium heat, add onions and garlic and cook for 3 minutes or until golden. Set aside.

2   Arrange lettuce, shallots, pork, prawns, chicken and peanuts attractively on a serving platter.

3   To make dressing, place sugar, fish sauce and lime juice in a bowl and mix to combine. Drizzle dressing over salad, then scatter with onion mixture and rose petals. Serve immediately.

*Serves 4*

When using rose petals in cooking check that they have not been sprayed with insecticides.

# THAI BEEF SALAD

500 g/1 lb rump or topside steak
185 g/6 oz mixed lettuce leaves
185 g/6 oz cherry tomatoes, halved
2 cucumbers, peeled and chopped
2 red onions, sliced
3 tablespoons fresh mint leaves

### LIME AND CORIANDER DRESSING

1 stalk fresh lemon grass, chopped or
1 teaspoon finely grated lemon rind
3 tablespoons fresh coriander leaves
1 tablespoon brown sugar
2 tablespoons lime juice
3 tablespoons light soy sauce
2 tablespoons sweet chilli sauce
2 teaspoons Thai fish sauce (nam pla)

When making a Thai salad, presentation is all important and a salad can be a spectacular centrepiece for any table. Traditionally Thai salads are served on flat plates – not in bowls – which means the full effect of the arrangement of ingredients can be appreciated.

1 Heat a frying or char-grill pan over a high heat until hot, add beef and cook for 1-2 minutes each side or until cooked to your liking. Set aside to cool.

2 Arrange lettuce, tomatoes, cucumbers, onions and mint attractively on a serving platter.

3 To make dressing, place lemon grass or rind, coriander, sugar, lime juice and soy, chilli and fish sauces in a bowl and mix to combine.

4 Slice beef thinly and arrange on salad, then drizzle with dressing and serve.

*Serves 4*

# CELLOPHANE NOODLE SALAD

Above: Cellophane Noodle Salad
Left: Thai Beef Salad

155 g/5 oz cellophane noodles
2 teaspoons sesame oil
2 cloves garlic, crushed
1 tablespoon finely grated fresh ginger
500 g/1 lb pork mince
15 g/¹/₂ oz mint leaves
15 g/¹/₂ oz coriander leaves
8 lettuce leaves
5 red or golden shallots, chopped
1 fresh red chilli, sliced
2 tablespoons lemon juice
1 tablespoon light soy sauce

1   Place noodles in a bowl and pour over boiling water to cover. Stand for 10 minutes, then drain well.

2   Heat oil in a frying pan over a high heat, add garlic and ginger and stir-fry for 1 minute. Add pork and stir-fry for 5 minutes or until pork is browned and cooked through.

3   Arrange mint, coriander, lettuce, shallots, chilli and noodles on a serving platter. Top with pork mixture, then drizzle with lemon juice and soy sauce.

*Serves 4*

Cellophane noodles also known as glass noodles and bean thread noodles or vermicelli are made from mung bean flour and are either very thin vermicelli-style noodles or flatter fettuccine-style noodles. In the dried state they are very tough and difficult to break. For ease of use it is best to buy a brand which packages them as bundles.

27

# PRAWN AND PAWPAW SALAD

2 teaspoons vegetable oil
2 teaspoons chilli paste (sambal oelek)
2 stalks fresh lemon grass, chopped,
or 1 teaspoon dried lemon grass,
soaked in hot water until soft
2 tablespoons shredded fresh ginger
500 g/1 lb medium uncooked prawns,
shelled and deveined
$^1/_2$ Chinese cabbage, shredded
4 red or golden shallots, chopped
1 pawpaw, peeled and sliced
60 g/2 oz watercress leaves
60 g/2 oz chopped roasted peanuts
30 g/1 oz fresh coriander leaves

LIME AND COCONUT DRESSING
1 teaspoon brown sugar
3 tablespoons lime juice
2 tablespoons Thai fish sauce (nam pla)
1 tablespoon coconut vinegar

1   Heat oil in a frying pan over a high heat, add chilli paste (sambal oelek), lemon grass and ginger and stir-fry for 1 minute. Add prawns and stir-fry for 2 minutes or until prawns change colour and are cooked through. Set aside to cool.

2   Arrange cabbage, shallots, pawpaw, watercress, peanuts, coriander and prawn mixture attractively on a serving platter.

3   To make dressing, place sugar, lime juice, fish sauce and vinegar in a bowl and mix to combine. Drizzle dressing over salad and serve.

*Serves 4*

Chinese cabbage is delicately flavoured with broad leaves and a closely packed head.

---

# BARBECUED SQUID SALAD

1 tablespoon chilli oil
1 tablespoon finely grated lemon rind
2 teaspoons crushed black
peppercorns
500 g/1 lb small squid (calamari)
hoods, cleaned
30 g/1 oz fresh basil leaves
30 g/1 oz fresh mint leaves
30 g/1 oz fresh coriander leaves

LEMON AND CHILLI DRESSING
1 fresh green chilli, chopped
2 tablespoons brown sugar
3 tablespoons lemon juice
2 tablespoons light soy sauce

1   Place oil, lemon rind and peppercorns in a shallow dish and mix to combine. Add squid (calamari) and marinate for 30 minutes.

2   Line a serving platter with the basil, mint and coriander. Cover with plastic food wrap and refrigerate until ready to serve.

3   To make dressing, place chilli, sugar, lemon juice and soy sauce in a bowl and mix to combine.

4   Preheat a barbecue, char-grill pan or frying pan and cook squid (calamari) for 30 seconds each side or until tender – take care not to overcook or the squid (calamari) will become tough. Place squid (calamari) on top of herbs and drizzle with dressing.

*Serves 4*

To clean squid (calamari), pull tentacles from the squid (calamari), carefully taking with them the stomach and ink bag. Next cut the beak, stomach and ink bag from the tentacles and discard. Wash tentacles well. Wash 'hood' and peel away skin. For this recipe, the hoods are left whole, if you wish the tentacles can be cut into small pieces and also used.

*Prawn and Pawpaw Salad,
Barbecued Squid Salad*

# STIR-FRIES

# CHICKEN WITH CHILLI JAM

*Previous pages: Chicken with Chilli Jam, Beef with Peppercorns*

2 teaspoons vegetable oil
3 chicken breast fillets or 4 boneless thigh fillets, cut into thin strips
4 red or golden shallots, chopped
185 g/6 oz broccoli, chopped
125 g/4 oz snow peas (mangetout), halved
60 g/2 oz unsalted, roasted cashews
2 tablespoons light soy sauce

CHILLI JAM
2 teaspoons vegetable oil
4 fresh red chillies, sliced
1 tablespoon shredded fresh ginger
1 teaspoon shrimp paste
$^1/_3$ cup/90 g/3 oz sugar
$^1/_3$ cup/90 mL/3 fl oz water
2 tablespoons lime juice

Serve this tasty chicken dish with steamed jasmine rice. If you prefer, the Chilli Jam can be served separately so that each diner can season their serving according to individual taste.

1  To make jam, heat oil in a wok over a medium heat, add chillies, ginger and shrimp paste and stir-fry for 1 minute or until golden. Stir in sugar, water and lime juice and cook, stirring, for 3 minutes or until mixture is thick. Remove jam from wok and set aside.

2  Heat oil in a clean wok over a high heat for 1 minute, add chicken and shallots and stir-fry for 3 minutes or until chicken is lightly browned.

3  Add broccoli, snow peas (mangetout), cashews and soy sauce and stir-fry for 3 minutes longer or until vegetables change colour and are cooked.

4  To serve, place chicken on serving plate and top with Chilli Jam.

*Serves 4*

# BEEF WITH PEPPERCORNS

2 teaspoons vegetable oil
2 cloves garlic, crushed
1 fresh green chilli, chopped
500 g/1 lb topside or round steak, sliced
1 tablespoon green peppercorns in brine, drained and lightly crushed
1 green pepper, chopped
3 tablespoons fresh coriander leaves
$^1/_3$ cup/90 mL/3 fl oz coconut milk
2 teaspoons Thai fish sauce (nam pla)

Black peppercorns are a traditional Thai ingredient and before the introduction of chillies by the Portuguese, they were used to add heat to dishes. This spicy stir-fry teams milder green peppercorns with chilli to make the most of two favourite ingredients.

1  Heat oil in a wok over a high heat. Add garlic and chilli and cook for 1 minute. Add beef and peppercorns and stir-fry for 3 minutes or until beef is browned.

2  Stir in green pepper, coriander, coconut milk and fish sauce and cook for 2 minutes longer.

*Serves 4*

*Coconut Prawns and Scallops*

# COCONUT PRAWNS AND SCALLOPS

1 kg/2 lb large uncooked prawns,
shelled and deveined, tails left intact
3 egg whites, lightly beaten
90 g/3 oz shredded coconut
vegetable oil for deep-frying
1 tablespoon peanut oil
4 fresh red chillies, seeded and sliced
2 small fresh green chillies, seeded
and sliced
2 cloves garlic, crushed
1 tablespoon shredded fresh ginger
3 kaffir lime leaves, finely shredded
375 g/12 oz scallops
125 g/4 oz snow pea (mangetout)
leaves or sprouts
2 tablespoons palm or brown sugar
$^1/_4$ cup/60 mL/2 fl oz lime juice
2 tablespoons Thai fish sauce (nam pla)

1   Dip prawns in egg whites, then roll
in coconut to coat. Heat vegetable oil
in a large saucepan until a cube of
bread dropped in browns in 50 seconds
and cook prawns, a few at a time, for
2-3 minutes or until golden and crisp.
Drain on absorbent kitchen paper and
keep warm.

2   Heat peanut oil in a wok over a
high heat, add red and green chillies,
garlic, ginger and lime leaves and stir-
fry for 2-3 minutes or until fragrant.

3   Add scallops to wok and stir-fry for
3 minutes or until opaque. Add cooked
prawns, snow pea (mangetout) leaves or
sprouts, sugar, lime juice and fish sauce
and stir-fry for 2 minutes or until heated.

*Serves 6*

If snow pea (mangetout)
leaves or sprouts are
unavailable watercress is a
good alternative for this dish.

33

# PORK AND PUMPKIN STIR-FRY

2 tablespoons Thai red curry paste
2 onions, cut into thin wedges,
layers separated
2 teaspoons vegetable oil
500 g/1 lb lean pork strips
500 g/1 lb peeled butternut pumpkin
(squash), cut into 2 cm/³/4 in cubes
4 kaffir lime leaves, shredded
1 tablespoon palm or brown sugar
2 cups/500 mL/16 fl oz coconut milk
1 tablespoon Thai fish sauce (nam pla)

1  Place curry paste in wok and cook,
stirring, over a high heat for 2 minutes
or until fragrant. Add onions and cook
for 2 minutes longer or until onions are
soft. Remove from pan and set aside.

2  Heat oil in wok, add pork and
stir-fry for 3 minutes or until brown.
Remove pork from pan and set aside.

3  Add pumpkin, lime leaves, sugar,
coconut milk and fish sauce to pan,
bring to simmering and simmer for
2 minutes. Stir in curry paste mixture
and simmer for 5 minutes longer. Return
pork to pan and cook for 2 minutes or
until heated.

*Serves 4*

Spoons and forks are used in
Thailand for eating, not
chopsticks. Like us, Thais
would only use chopsticks
when eating Chinese food.

# PORK WITH GARLIC AND PEPPER

2 teaspoons vegetable oil
4 cloves garlic, sliced
1 tablespoon crushed black
peppercorns
500 g/1 lb lean pork strips
1 bunch/500 g/1 lb baby bok choy
(Chinese greens), chopped
4 tablespoons fresh coriander leaves
2 tablespoons palm or brown sugar
2 tablespoons light soy sauce
2 tablespoons lime juice

1  Heat oil in a wok or frying pan over
a medium heat, add garlic and black
peppercorns and stir-fry for 1 minute.
Add pork and stir-fry for 3 minutes or
until brown.

2  Add bok choy (Chinese greens),
coriander, sugar, soy sauce and lime
juice and stir-fry for 3-4 minutes or
until pork and bok choy are tender.

*Serves 4*

Bok choy is also known as
Chinese chard, buck choy
and pak choi. It varies in
length from 10-30 cm/4-12 in.
For this recipe the smaller
variety is used. It has a mild,
cabbage-like flavour.
Ordinary cabbage could
be used for this recipe.

*Pork with Garlic and Pepper,
Pork and Pumpkin Stir-fry*

# STIR-FRIED DUCK WITH GREENS

Chinese broccoli (gai lum) is a popular Asian vegetable. It has dark green leaves on firm stalks often with small white flowers. The leaves, stalks and flowers are all used in cooking, however the stalks are considered to be the choicest part of the plant. To prepare, remove leaves from stalks and peel, then chop both leaves and stalks and use as directed in the recipe.

1.2 kg/2$^1$/$_2$ lb Chinese barbecued or roasted duck
2 teaspoons vegetable oil
1 tablespoon Thai red curry paste
1 teaspoon shrimp paste
1 stalk fresh lemon grass, finely sliced, or $^1$/$_2$ teaspoon dried lemon grass, soaked in hot water until soft
4 fresh red chillies
1 bunch Chinese broccoli (gai lum) or Swiss chard, chopped
1 tablespoon palm or brown sugar
2 tablespoons tamarind concentrate
1 tablespoon Thai fish sauce (nam pla)

1   Slice meat from duck, leaving the skin on, and cut into bite-sized pieces. Reserve as many of the cavity juices as possible.

2   Heat oil in a wok over a medium heat, add curry paste, shrimp paste, lemon grass and chillies and stir-fry for 3 minutes or until fragrant.

3   Add duck and reserved juices and stir-fry for 2 minutes or until coated in spice mixture and heated. Add broccoli or chard, sugar, tamarind and fish sauce and stir-fry for 3-4 minutes or until broccoli is wilted.

*Serves 4*

# BEEF AND BEAN STIR-FRY

*Above: Beef and Bean Stir-fry*
*Left: Stir-fried Duck with Greens*

2 teaspoons vegetable oil
2 cloves garlic, crushed
500 g/1 lb topside or round steak, cut
into thin strips
185 g/6 oz snake (yard-long) or green
beans, cut into 10 cm/4 in lengths
2 kaffir lime leaves, shredded
2 teaspoons brown sugar
2 tablespoons light soy sauce
1 tablespoon Thai fish sauce (nam pla)
2 tablespoons coriander leaves

1  Heat oil and garlic together in a wok over a medium heat, increase heat to high, add beef and stir-fry for 3 minutes or until beef changes colour.

2  Add beans, lime leaves, sugar and soy and fish sauces and stir-fry for 2 minutes or until beans change colour. Stir in coriander and serve immediately.

*Serves 4*

Kaffir limes are a popular Thai ingredient. Both the fruit and the leaves have a distinctive flavour and perfume and are used in cooking. The leaves are available dried, fresh frozen or fresh from Oriental food shops and some greengrocers. If kaffir lime leaves are unavailable a little finely grated lime rind can be used instead.

# STIR-FRIED BITTER MELON

This dish is delicious served on a bed of cellophane noodles and topped with fried onions. Bitter melon (gourd) looks somewhat like a cucumber with a lumpy skin and as the name suggests has a bitter taste. It should always be degorged with salt before using.

1 medium bitter melon (gourd), peeled, seeds removed, cut into 1 cm/$^1$/2 in thick slices
2 tablespoons salt
1 tablespoon vegetable oil
3 tablespoons small dried prawns
6 red or golden shallots, sliced
2 cloves garlic, sliced
2 stalks fresh lemon grass, finely sliced, or 1 teaspoon finely grated lemon rind
3 fresh green chillies, finely sliced
1 small red pawpaw, cut into 3 cm/1$^1$/4 in cubes
125 g/4 oz snow peas (mangetout), halved
1 tablespoon tamarind concentrate

1   Rub each slice of bitter melon (gourd) with salt, place in a colander and set aside for 30 minutes. Rinse under cold water and drain thoroughly.

2   Heat oil in a wok over a medium heat, add dried prawns, shallots, garlic and lemon grass or rind and stir-fry for 4 minutes or until shallots are golden.

3   Add chillies and bitter melon (gourd) and stir-fry for 4 minutes or until melon is tender. Add pawpaw, snow peas (mangetout) and tamarind and stir-fry for 2 minutes or until snow peas (mangetout) are tender.

*Serves 4*

# EGGPLANT AND BASIL STIR-FRY

Stir-frying is a very quick cooking process – this dish takes less than 10 minutes – it is therefore very important that all preparation such as cutting and chopping have been completed before the cooking starts.

3 eggplant (aubergines), halved lengthways and cut into 1 cm/$^1$/2 in thick slices
salt
1 tablespoon vegetable oil
2 onions, cut into thin wedges, layers separated
3 fresh red chillies, chopped
2 cloves garlic, sliced
1 stalk fresh lemon grass, chopped, or $^1$/2 teaspoon dried lemon grass, soaked in hot water until soft
250 g/8 oz green beans, trimmed
1 cup/250 mL/8 fl oz coconut cream
45 g/1$^1$/2 oz basil leaves

1   Place eggplant (aubergines) in a colander, sprinkle with salt and set aside for 20 minutes. Rinse under cold running water and pat dry on absorbent kitchen paper.

2   Heat oil in a wok or frying pan over a high heat, add onions, chillies, garlic and lemon grass and stir-fry for 3 minutes. Add eggplant (aubergines), beans and coconut cream and stir-fry for 5 minutes or until eggplant (aubergines) are tender. Stir in basil.

*Serves 6*

*Stir-fried Bitter Melon,*
*Eggplant and Basil Stir-fry*

Above: Stir-fried Tamarind Prawns
Right: Mussels with Coconut
Vinegar

# STIR-FRIED TAMARIND PRAWNS

Tamarind is the large pod of the tamarind or Indian date tree. After picking, it is seeded and peeled, then pressed into a dark brown pulp. It is also available as a concentrate. Tamarind pulp or concentrate can be purchased from Indian food stores. In Oriental cooking it is used as a souring agent, if unavailable a mixture of lime or lemon juice and treacle can be used instead.

2 tablespoons tamarind pulp
$^1/_2$ cup/125 mL/4 fl oz water
2 teaspoons vegetable oil
3 stalks fresh lemon grass, chopped,
or 2 teaspoons finely grated lemon rind
2 fresh red chillies, chopped
500 g/1 lb medium uncooked prawns,
shelled and deveined, tails intact
2 green (unripe) mangoes, peeled
and thinly sliced
3 tablespoons chopped fresh coriander
leaves
2 tablespoons brown sugar
2 tablespoons lime juice

1   Place tamarind pulp and water in a bowl and stand for 20 minutes. Strain, reserve liquid and set aside. Discard solids.

2   Heat oil in a wok or frying pan over a high heat, add lemon grass or rind and chillies and stir-fry for 1 minute. Add prawns and stir-fry for 2 minutes or until they change colour.

3   Add mangoes, coriander, sugar, lime juice and tamarind liquid and stir-fry for 5 minutes or until prawns are cooked.

*Serves 4*

40

# MUSSELS WITH COCONUT VINEGAR

1.5 kg/3 lb mussels in their shells
6 whole coriander plants, washed and
roughly chopped
3 stalks fresh lemon grass, bruised, or
1¹/₂ teaspoons dried lemon grass,
soaked in hot water until soft
5 cm/2 in piece fresh ginger, shredded
¹/₂ cup/125 mL/4 fl oz water
1 tablespoon vegetable oil
1 red onion, halved and sliced
2 fresh red chillies, sliced
2 tablespoons coconut vinegar
fresh coriander leaves

1   Place mussels, coriander, lemon
grass, ginger and water in a wok over a
high heat. Cover and cook for 5 minutes
or until mussels open. Discard any
mussels that do not open after 5 minutes
cooking. Remove mussels from wok,
discard coriander, lemon grass and ginger.
Strain cooking liquid and reserve.

2   Heat oil in a wok over a medium
heat, add onion and chillies and stir-fry
for 3 minutes or until onion is soft.
Add mussels, reserved cooking liquid
and coconut vinegar and stir-fry for
2 minutes or until mussels are heated.
Scatter with coriander leaves and serve.

*Serves 4*

This dish is delicious served
with boiled egg noodles
and topped with coriander
leaves and wok juices.
Coconut vinegar is made
from the sap of the coconut
palm. It is available from
Oriental food shops. If
unavailable any mild vinegar
can be used instead.

# CURRIES

# CARDAMOM AND ORANGE DUCK

1.5 kg/3 lb Chinese barbecued or
roasted duck
3 cups/750 mL/1¼ pt chicken stock
2 small fresh red chillies, halved
3 cm/1¼ in piece fresh galangal or
ginger, sliced, or 5 slices bottled
galangal
2 stalks fresh lemon grass, cut into
3 cm/1¼ in pieces, bruised, or
1 teaspoon dried lemon grass, soaked
in hot water until soft
6 whole coriander plants, washed,
stems and roots removed, leaves
reserved
6 cardamom pods, crushed
4 kaffir lime leaves, torn into pieces
1 large orange, peeled, all white pith
removed from rind, flesh segmented
and reserved
1 tablespoon vegetable oil
2 teaspoons shrimp paste
2 teaspoons Thai red curry paste
1 clove garlic, finely chopped
1 tablespoon palm or brown sugar
2 spring onions, cut into thin strips

1   Remove meat from duck and cut into bite-sized pieces – reserve bones, skin and as many of the juices as possible. Place reserved bones, skin and juices, stock, chillies, galangal or ginger, lemon grass, coriander stems and roots, cardamom pods, lime leaves and orange rind in a saucepan and bring to the boil. Reduce heat and simmer, uncovered, for 15 minutes. Strain liquid and set aside. Discard solids.

2   Heat oil in a wok or large saucepan over a medium heat, add shrimp and curry pastes and garlic and cook, stirring, for 1-2 minutes or until fragrant.

3   Add duck pieces and stir to coat with spice paste. Add reserved liquid and simmer for 3-4 minutes or until liquid reduces slightly. Stir in orange segments, coriander leaves and sugar. Serve scattered with spring onions.

*Serves 4*

Chinese barbecued or roasted duck is available from Oriental food stores which sell meat. If unavailable roast duck can be used instead.

# THAI GREEN CHICKEN CURRY

1 tablespoon vegetable oil
2 onions, chopped
3 tablespoons Thai green curry paste
1 kg/2 lb boneless chicken thigh or
breast fillets, chopped
4 tablespoons fresh basil leaves
6 kaffir lime leaves, shredded
2½ cups/600 mL/1 pt coconut milk
2 tablespoons Thai fish sauce (nam pla)
extra fresh basil leaves

1   Heat oil in a saucepan over a high heat, add onions and cook for 3 minutes or until golden. Stir in curry paste and cook for 2 minutes or until fragrant.

2   Add chicken, basil, lime leaves, coconut milk and fish sauce and bring to the boil. Reduce heat and simmer for 12-15 minutes or until chicken is tender and sauce is thick. Serve garnished with extra basil.

*Serves 6*

The curry pastes of Thailand are mixtures of freshly ground herbs and spices and if you are able to make your own it is well worth the small effort required. Recipes for Thai green and red curry pastes can be found in the Glossary on page 78.

*Minted Bean Curry*

# MINTED BEAN CURRY

6 whole coriander plants, roots
removed and washed, reserve leaves
for another use
2 stalks fresh lemon grass, finely
sliced, or 1 teaspoon dried lemon
grass, soaked in hot water until soft
6 kaffir lime leaves, shredded
2 teaspoons palm or brown sugar
3 cups/750 mL/1$^1$/$_4$ pt water
3 tablespoons Thai fish sauce (nam pla)
2 teaspoons peanut oil
3 small fresh green chillies, shredded
(optional)
5 cm/2 in piece fresh ginger, shredded
2 teaspoons Thai green curry paste
220 g/7 oz pea eggplant (aubergines)
220 g/7 oz snake (yard-long) or green
beans, cut into 2.5 cm/1 in pieces
440 g/14 oz canned tomatoes, drained
and chopped
2 tablespoons tamarind concentrate
60 g/2 oz fresh mint leaves

1  Place coriander roots, lemon grass,
lime leaves, sugar, water and fish sauce
in a saucepan and bring to the boil.
Reduce heat and simmer for 10 minutes.
Strain, discard solids and set stock aside.

2  Heat oil in a wok or large saucepan
over a medium heat, add chillies (if
using), ginger and curry paste and stir-
fry for 2-3 minutes or until fragrant.
Add eggplant (aubergines) and beans
and stir to coat with spice mixture. Stir
in reserved stock and simmer for
10 minutes or until vegetables are
tender. Add tomatoes and tamarind
and simmer for 3 minutes or until hot.
Stir in mint.

*Serves 4*

Pea eggplant (aubergines)
are tiny green eggplant
(aubergines) about the size
of green peas and are
usually purchased still
attached to the vine. They
are used whole, eaten raw
or cooked and have a bitter
taste. If unavailable green
peas can be used instead.

# CASHEW AND CHILLI BEEF CURRY

3 cm/1¼ in piece fresh galangal or ginger, chopped or 5 slices bottled galangal, chopped
1 stalk fresh lemon grass, finely sliced, or ½ teaspoon dried lemon grass, soaked in hot water until soft
3 kaffir lime leaves, finely shredded
2 small fresh red chillies, seeded and chopped
2 teaspoons shrimp paste
2 tablespoons Thai fish sauce (nam pla)
1 tablespoon lime juice
2 tablespoons peanut oil
4 red or golden shallots, sliced
2 cloves garlic, chopped
3 small fresh red chillies, sliced
500 g/1 lb round or blade steak, cut into 2 cm/¾ in cubes
2 cups/500 mL/16 fl oz beef stock
250 g/8 oz okra, trimmed
60 g/2 oz cashews, roughly chopped
1 tablespoon palm or brown sugar
2 tablespoons light soy sauce

1  Place galangal or ginger, lemon grass, lime leaves, chopped chillies, shrimp paste, fish sauce and lime juice in a food processor and process to make a thick paste, adding a little water if necessary.

2  Heat 1 tablespoon oil in a wok or large saucepan over a medium heat, add shallots, garlic, sliced red chillies and spice paste and cook, stirring, for 2-3 minutes or until fragrant. Remove and set aside.

3  Heat remaining oil in wok over a high heat and stir-fry beef, in batches, until brown. Return spice paste to pan, stir in stock and okra and bring to the boil. Reduce heat and simmer, stirring occasionally, for 15 minutes.

4  Stir in cashews, sugar and soy sauce and simmer for 10 minutes longer or until beef is tender.

*Serves 4*

Fish sauce 'nam pla' is characteristic of Thai cooking and appears as a seasoning in many dishes. Thai cooks take pride in making their own fish sauce and the ability to make a good sauce is the hallmark of an accomplished cook.

# RED BEEF CURRY

1 cup/250 mL/8 fl oz coconut cream
3 tablespoons Thai red curry paste
500 g/1 lb round or blade steak, cubed
155 g/5 oz pea eggplant (aubergines) or 1 eggplant (aubergine), diced
220 g/7 oz canned sliced bamboo shoots
6 kaffir lime leaves, crushed
1 tablespoon brown sugar
2 cups/500 mL/16 fl oz coconut milk
2 tablespoons Thai fish sauce (nam pla)
3 tablespoons fresh coriander leaves
2 fresh red chillies, chopped

1  Place coconut cream in a saucepan and bring to the boil over a high heat, then boil until oil separates from coconut cream and it reduces and thickens slightly. Stir in curry paste and boil for 2 minutes or until fragrant.

2  Add beef, eggplant (aubergines), bamboo shoots, lime leaves, sugar, coconut milk and fish sauce, cover and simmer for 35-40 minutes or until beef is tender. Stir in coriander and chillies.

*Serves 4*

In Thailand curries are usually served over moulds of rice. The rice absorbs and is flavoured by the large proportion of liquid in the curry. The fragrant rices such as jasmine and basmati are perfect accompaniments for Thai curries.

*Red Beef Curry, Cashew and Chilli Beef Curry*

# SWEET POTATO AND TOFU CURRY

1 tablespoon peanut oil
1 teaspoon chilli oil (optional)
315 g/10 oz firm tofu, cut into
1 cm/$^1$/$_2$ in thick slices
1$^1$/$_2$ cups/375 mL/12 fl oz coconut
cream
1 cup/250 mL/8 fl oz vegetable stock
2 teaspoons Thai red curry paste
375 g/12 oz sweet potato, cut into
2 cm/$^3$/$_4$ in cubes
2 teaspoons palm or brown sugar
1 tablespoon Thai fish sauce (nam pla)
2 teaspoons lime juice
60 g/2 oz fresh basil leaves

This vegetarian curry is delicious served over cellophane noodles. The fish sauce may be replaced with light soy sauce if you wish.

1   Heat peanut oil and chilli oil (if using) in a wok or large saucepan over a medium heat, add tofu and stir-fry until brown on all sides. Remove, drain on absorbent kitchen paper and set aside.

2   Using absorbent kitchen paper, wipe wok or saucepan clean, then add coconut cream and stock and bring to the boil. Stir in curry paste and cook for 3-4 minutes or until fragrant.

3   Add sweet potato, cover and cook over a medium heat for 8-10 minutes or until sweet potato is almost cooked.

4   Stir in sugar, fish sauce and lime juice and cook for 4-5 minutes longer or until sweet potato is tender. Stir in basil.

*Serves 4*

# PORK AND PINEAPPLE WITH BASIL

4 red or golden shallots, chopped
2 fresh red chillies, finely chopped
3 cm/1¹/4 in piece fresh galangal or
ginger, finely chopped, or 5 slices
bottled galangal, chopped
4 kaffir lime leaves
1 stalk fresh lemon grass, tender
white part only, finely sliced, or
¹/2 teaspoon dried lemon grass, soaked
in hot water until soft
1 tablespoon tamarind concentrate
2 tablespoons lime juice
1 tablespoon water
2 teaspoons shrimp paste
1 tablespoon dried shrimps
350 g/11 oz pork fillets, cut into
3 cm/1¹/4 in cubes
1 tablespoon vegetable oil
1 teaspoon palm or brown sugar
1¹/2 cups/375 mL/12 fl oz coconut
cream
¹/2 cup/125 mL/4 fl oz coconut milk
2 tablespoons Thai fish sauce (nam pla)
¹/2 small (about 200 g/6¹/2 oz) fresh
pineapple, cut into 2 cm/³/4 in wide
strips
60 g/2 oz fresh basil leaves

1  Place shallots, chillies, galangal
or ginger, lime leaves, lemon grass,
tamarind, 1 tablespoon lime juice,
water, shrimp paste and dried shrimps
in a food processor and process to make
a thick paste, adding a little more water
if necessary.

2  Place pork in a bowl, add spice paste
and toss to coat pork well.

3  Heat oil in a wok or large saucepan
over a medium heat, add pork and
stir-fry for 5 minutes or until fragrant
and pork is just cooked.

4  Stir in sugar, coconut cream and
milk and fish sauce and simmer,
uncovered, for 8-10 minutes or until
pork is tender.

5  Add pineapple and remaining lime
juice and simmer for 3 minutes or until
pineapple is heated. Stir in basil.

*Serves 4*

When handling fresh chillies,
do not put your hands near
your eyes or allow them to
touch your lips. To avoid
discomfort and burning, you
might like to wear gloves.
Chillies are also available
minced in jars from
supermarkets.

*Above left: Sweet Potato and Tofu Curry*
*Right: Pork and Pineapple with Basil*

# GREEN MANGO AND FISH CURRY

1¹/₂ cups/375 mL/12 fl oz coconut
cream
1 teaspoon Thai green curry paste
1 stalk fresh lemon grass, bruised, or
¹/₂ teaspoon dried lemon grass, soaked
in hot water until soft
4 kaffir lime leaves, finely sliced
1 large green (unripe) mango, cut into
5 mm/¹/₄ in thick slices
500 g/1 lb firm fish fillets, cut into
5 cm/2 in cubes
1 tablespoon palm or brown sugar
2 tablespoons Thai fish sauce (nam pla)
1 tablespoon coconut vinegar
60 g/2 oz fresh coriander leaves

Green (unripe) mango and
pawpaw are commonly
used in Thai cooking, they
add a tartness to the finished
dish. If green (unripe)
mangoes are unavailable,
use very tart green apples,
but on no account use ripe
mangoes as they do not give
the same flavour or texture.

1   Place coconut cream, curry paste,
lemon grass and lime leaves in a
saucepan and bring to the boil, reduce
heat and simmer for 5 minutes or until
fragrant.

2   Add mango and simmer for 3 minutes.
Add fish, sugar and fish sauce and
simmer for 3-4 minutes or until fish is
cooked. Stir in vinegar and coriander.

*Serves 4*

# GREEN CHILLI AND PRAWN CURRY

1 tablespoon vegetable oil
1.5 kg/3 lb medium uncooked prawns,
shelled and deveined, shells and heads
reserved
2 stalks fresh lemon grass, bruised, or
1 teaspoon dried lemon grass, soaked
in hot water until soft
2 long fresh green chillies, halved
4 cm/1¹/₂ in piece fresh galangal or
ginger, or 6 slices bottled galangal
3 cups/750 mL/1¹/₄ pt water
2 teaspoons Thai green curry paste
1 cucumber, seeded and cut
into thin strips
5 whole fresh green chillies (optional)
1 tablespoon palm or brown sugar
2 tablespoons Thai fish sauce (nam pla)
1 tablespoon coconut vinegar
2 teaspoons tamarind concentrate

Fresh lemon grass is available
from Oriental food shops
and some supermarkets and
greengrocers. It is also
available dried; if using dried
lemon grass soak it in hot
water for 20 minutes or until
soft before using. Lemon
grass is also available in
bottles from supermarkets,
use this in the same way as
you would fresh lemon grass.

1   Heat 2 teaspoons oil in a saucepan
over a medium heat, add reserved
prawn shells and heads and cook,
stirring, for 3-4 minutes or until shells
change colour. Add lemon grass, the
halved green chillies, galangal or ginger
and water and bring to the boil. Using
a wooden spoon break up galangal or
ginger, reduce heat and simmer for
10 minutes. Strain, discard solids and
set stock aside.

2   Heat remaining oil in a wok or
saucepan over a medium heat and
stir-fry curry paste for 2-3 minutes or
until fragrant.

3   Add prawns, cucumber, 5 whole
green chillies (if using), sugar, reserved
stock, fish sauce, vinegar and tamarind
and cook, stirring, for 4-5 minutes or
until prawns change colour and are
cooked through.

*Serves 4*

# Chicken Phanaeng Curry

2 cups/500 mL/16 fl oz coconut milk
3 tablespoons Thai red curry paste
500 g/1 lb chicken breast fillets, sliced
250 g/8 oz snake (yard-long) or
green beans
3 tablespoons unsalted peanuts,
roasted and finely chopped
2 teaspoons brown or palm sugar
1 tablespoon Thai fish sauce (nam pla)
1/2 cup/125 mL/4 fl oz coconut cream
2 tablespoons fresh basil leaves
2 tablespoons fresh coriander leaves
sliced fresh red chilli

1   Place coconut milk in a saucepan and bring to the boil over a high heat, then boil until oil separates from coconut milk and it reduces and thickens slightly. Stir in curry paste and boil for 2 minutes or until fragrant.

2   Add chicken, beans, peanuts, sugar and fish sauce and simmer for 5-7 minutes or until chicken is tender. Stir in coconut cream, basil and coriander. Serve garnished with slices of chilli.

*Serves 4*

To store whole fresh coriander plants, place roots in 1 cm/ 1/2 in of water in a glass jar, cover coriander and jar with a plastic bag, secure bag around jar and store in the refrigerator. Coriander and other fresh herbs purchased in good condition will keep for a week or more when stored in this way. Do not wash the herbs before storing.

# Chicken with Lime and Coconut

1 kg/2 lb chicken thigh or breast
fillets, cut into thick strips
1 tablespoon Thai red curry paste
1 tablespoon vegetable oil
3 tablespoons palm or brown sugar
4 kaffir lime leaves
2 teaspoons finely grated lime rind
1 cup/250 mL/8 fl oz coconut cream
1 tablespoon Thai fish sauce (nam pla)
2 tablespoons coconut vinegar
3 tablespoons shredded coconut
4 fresh red chillies, sliced

1   Place chicken and curry paste in a bowl and toss to coat. Heat oil in a wok or large saucepan over a high heat, add chicken and stir-fry for 4-5 minutes or until lightly browned and fragrant.

2   Add sugar, lime leaves, lime rind, coconut cream and fish sauce and cook, stirring, over a medium heat for 3-4 minutes or until the sugar dissolves and caramelises.

3   Stir in vinegar and coconut and simmer until chicken is tender. Serve with chillies in a dish on the side.

*Serves 4*

For something a little different serve this dish with egg noodles.

*Chicken Phanaeng Curry,*
*Chicken with Lime and Coconut*

# STEAMED, GRILLED & FRIED

# DEEP-FRIED CHILLI FISH

**2 x 500 g/1 lb whole fish such as bream, snapper, whiting, sea perch, cod or haddock, cleaned**
**4 fresh red chillies, chopped**
**4 fresh coriander roots**
**3 cloves garlic, crushed**
**1 teaspoon crushed black peppercorns**
**vegetable oil for deep-frying**

RED CHILLI SAUCE
**$^2$/$_3$ cup/170 g/5$^1$/$_2$ oz sugar**
**8 fresh red chillies, sliced**
**4 red or golden shallots, sliced**
**$^1$/$_3$ cup/90 mL/3 fl oz coconut vinegar**
**$^1$/$_3$ cup/90 mL/3 fl oz water**

This dish is a stunning centrepiece for a Thai feast.

1   Make diagonal slashes along both sides of the fish.

2   Place chopped chillies, coriander roots, garlic and black peppercorns in a food processor and process to make a paste. Spread mixture over both sides of fish and marinate for 30 minutes.

3   To make sauce, place sugar, sliced chillies, shallots, vinegar and water in a saucepan and cook, stirring, over a low heat until sugar dissolves. Bring mixture to simmering and simmer, stirring occasionally, for 4 minutes or until sauce thickens.

4   Heat vegetable oil in a wok or deep-frying pan until a cube of bread dropped in browns in 50 seconds. Cook fish, one at a time, for 2 minutes each side or until crisp and flesh flakes when tested with a fork. Drain on absorbent kitchen paper. Serve with chilli sauce.

*Serves 6*

# FISH WITH GREEN MANGO SAUCE

Oven temperature
180°C, 350°F, Gas 4 (optional)

Banana leaves are used in South-East Asian and Pacific countries in much the same way as Westerners use aluminium foil. Foil can be used if banana leaves are unavailable, however the finished dish will not have the flavour that the banana leaf contributes and it may be slightly drier. See Glossary on page 78 for preparation and blanching information.

**4 x 185 g/6 oz firm fish fillets or cutlets**
**4 pieces banana leaf, blanched**
**3 cloves garlic, sliced**
**1 tablespoon shredded fresh ginger**
**2 kaffir lime leaves, shredded**

GREEN MANGO SAUCE
**$^1$/$_2$ small green (unripe) mango, flesh grated**
**3 red or golden shallots, chopped**
**2 fresh red chillies, sliced**
**1 tablespoon brown sugar**
**$^1$/$_4$ cup/60 mL/2 fl oz water**
**1 tablespoon Thai fish sauce (nam pla)**

1   Place a fish fillet or cutlet in the centre of each banana leaf. Top fish with a little each of the garlic, ginger and lime leaves, then fold over banana leaves to enclose. Place parcels over a charcoal barbecue or bake in the oven for 15-20 minutes or until fish flakes when tested with a fork.

2   To make sauce, place mango, shallots, chillies, sugar, water and fish sauce in a saucepan and cook, stirring, over a low heat for 4-5 minutes or until sauce is heated through.

3   To serve, place parcels on serving plates, cut open to expose fish and serve with sauce.

*Serves 4*

# SHELLFISH WITH LEMON GRASS

5 red or golden shallots, chopped
4 stalks fresh lemon grass, bruised
and cut into 3 cm/1$^1$/$_4$ in pieces, or
2 teaspoons dried lemon grass, soaked
in hot water until soft
3 cloves garlic, chopped
5 cm/2 in piece fresh ginger, shredded
3 fresh red chillies, seeded and chopped
8 kaffir lime leaves, torn into pieces
750 g/1$^1$/$_2$ lb mussels, scrubbed and
beards removed
$^1$/$_4$ cup/60 mL/2 fl oz water
12 scallops on shells, cleaned
1 tablespoon lime juice
1 tablespoon Thai fish sauce (nam pla)
3 tablespoons fresh basil leaves

1   Place shallots, lemon grass, garlic, ginger, chillies and lime leaves in a small bowl and mix to combine.

2   Place mussels in a wok and sprinkle over half the shallot mixture. Pour in water, cover and cook over a high heat for 5 minutes.

3   Add scallops, remaining shallot mixture, lime juice, fish sauce and basil and toss to combine. Cover and cook for 4-5 minutes or until mussels and scallops are cooked. Discard any mussels that do not open after 5 minutes.

*Serves 4*

Serve this dish at the table straight from the wok and don't forget to give each diner some of the delicious cooking juices.

# CHICKEN WITH GARLIC AND PEPPER

4 cloves garlic
3 fresh coriander roots
1 teaspoon crushed black peppercorns
500 g/1 lb chicken breast fillets,
chopped into 3 cm/1 1/4 in cubes
vegetable oil for deep-frying
30 g/1 oz fresh basil leaves
30 g/1 oz fresh mint leaves
sweet chilli sauce

Thai cooks use three types of
basil in cooking – Asian sweet,
holy and lemon – each has a
distinctive flavour and is used
for specific types of dishes.
For this dish Asian sweet
basil, known in Thailand as
horapa, would be used. For
more information about basil
see Glossary on page 78.

1   Place garlic, coriander roots and
black peppercorns in a food processor
and process to make a paste. Coat
chicken with garlic paste and marinate
for 1 hour.

2   Heat oil in a wok or frying pan over
a high heat until a cube of bread
dropped in browns in 50 seconds, then
deep-fry chicken, a few pieces at a time,
for 2 minutes or until golden and tender.
Drain on absorbent kitchen paper.

3   Deep-fry basil and mint until crisp,
then drain and place on a serving plate.
Top with chicken and serve with
chilli sauce.

*Serves 4*

# CHARCOAL-GRILLED CHICKEN

1 kg/2 lb chicken pieces
4 fresh red chillies, chopped
4 cloves garlic, chopped
3 fresh coriander roots, chopped
2 stalks fresh lemon grass, chopped,
or 1 teaspoon dried lemon grass
soaked in hot water until soft
3 tablespoons lime juice
2 tablespoons light soy sauce
1 cup/250 mL/8 fl oz coconut cream
sweet chilli sauce

Many Thai recipes such as
this one, and some of the
others in this chapter and in
the Snacks and Starters
chapter, are great for
barbecuing. For a
memorable Thai-inspired
barbecue meal, serve your
favourite Thai barbecue
dishes with a selection of
Thai-style salads and dipping
sauces. Other recipes
suitable for barbecuing
include Satay (page 8), Fish
with Green Mango Sauce
(page 56), Spiced Grilled
Beef (page 60) and
Barbecued Pork Spare Ribs
(page 61).

1   Place chicken in a ceramic or glass
dish and set aside.

2   Place chillies, garlic, coriander
roots, lemon grass, lime juice and soy
sauce in a food processor and process to
make paste. Mix paste with coconut
cream and pour over chicken. Marinate
for 1 hour.

3   Drain chicken and reserve marinade.
Cook chicken over a slow charcoal or
gas barbecue or under a preheated low
grill, brushing frequently with reserved
marinade, for 25-30 minutes or until
chicken is tender. Serve with chilli
sauce.

*Serves 6*

*Charcoal-grilled Chicken,
Chicken with Garlic and Pepper*

# Spiced Grilled Beef

Oven temperature
200°C, 400°F, Gas 6 (optional)

Rice is central to any Thai meal and steamed jasmine rice is the one most commonly eaten. To balance the salty flavours of the other dishes served at the meal, the rice is cooked unsalted and while the other dishes can be served at room temperature the rice should be served steaming hot.

1 red onion, chopped
4 cloves garlic, crushed
2 fresh coriander roots
1 teaspoon crushed black peppercorns
2 tablespoons light soy sauce
2 teaspoons lime juice
2 teaspoons Thai fish sauce (nam pla)
500 g/1 lb rib-eye (scotch fillet) of beef, in one piece
6 lettuce leaves
185 g/6 oz cherry tomatoes, halved
1 cucumber, cut into strips
lime wedges

1   Place onion, garlic, coriander roots, peppercorns, soy sauce, lime juice and fish sauce in a food processor and process to make a paste. Coat beef with spice mixture and cook over a medium charcoal or gas barbecue, turning occasionally, for 15 minutes or until beef is cooked to medium doneness. Alternatively, bake beef in oven for 30-45 minutes or until cooked to medium doneness.

2   Arrange lettuce, tomatoes and cucumber on a serving plate. Slice beef thinly and arrange over lettuce. Serve with lime wedges.

*Serves 4*

# BARBECUED PORK SPARE RIBS

*Above: Barbecued Pork Spare Ribs*
*Left: Spiced Grilled Beef*

4 cloves garlic, chopped
2 tablespoons finely grated fresh ginger
2 tablespoons sugar
2 teaspoons ground cumin
$^1/_2$ cup dark soy sauce
1 kg/2 lb pork belly spare ribs

1   Place garlic, ginger, sugar, cumin and soy sauce in a glass or ceramic bowl and mix to combine. Add spare ribs, turn to coat and marinate for 1 hour.

2   Drain ribs and reserve marinade. Cook ribs over a preheated hot barbecue or under a hot grill, basting frequently with marinade, for 15 minutes or until pork is cooked through and skin crackles.

*Serves 6*

For an informal meal, serve these tasty spare ribs with a salad of Asian greens and herbs and bowls of steamed jasmine rice.

# STEAMED FISH MOUSSE

banana leaves, blanched
2 cups/500 mL/16 fl oz coconut milk
3 tablespoons Thai red curry paste
2 eggs, lightly beaten
500 g/1 lb firm white fish fillets,
chopped
2 kaffir lime leaves, shredded
1 teaspoon sugar
2 tablespoons Thai fish sauce (nam pla)
125 g/4 oz fresh basil leaves
1/2 cup/125 mL/4 fl oz coconut cream

1   Cut six 20 cm/8 in circles from the
banana leaves. Make four pinch pleats
around the edge of the circle and secure
with a toothpick to make a cup. Set aside.

2   Place 1 cup/250 mL/8 fl oz coconut
milk in a saucepan and bring to the
boil. Stir in curry paste and mix to

combine. Remove from heat, cool
slightly, then whisk in eggs. Add fish,
lime leaves, sugar, fish sauce and
remaining coconut milk and cook,
stirring, over a low heat for 5 minutes.

3   Sprinkle the base of banana leaf
cups with basil, then divide fish
mixture evenly between cups. Place
cups in a bamboo steamer and set aside.

4   Half fill a wok with hot water and
bring to the boil. Place steamer on a
wire rack in wok, cover and steam for
15 minutes. Top each mousse with a
little coconut cream, then steam for
5-7 minutes longer or until mousse
are firm.

*Serves 6*

If banana leaves are not
available 1 cup/250 mL/8 fl oz
capacity ramekins can be
used instead.

---

# FISH WITH LIME AND GARLIC

750 g/1 1/2 lb whole fish such as sea
perch, sea bass, coral trout or snapper,
cleaned
2 stalks fresh lemon grass, chopped,
or 1 teaspoon dried lemon grass,
soaked in hot water until soft
4 slices fresh ginger
1 fresh green chilli, halved
4 kaffir lime leaves, crushed
8 whole fresh coriander plants

LIME AND GARLIC SAUCE
2 fresh red chillies, seeded and chopped
2 green chillies, seeded and chopped
3 cloves garlic, chopped
1 tablespoon shredded fresh ginger
1 cup/250 mL/8 fl oz fish or
chicken stock
4 tablespoons lime juice
1 tablespoon Thai fish sauce (nam pla)

1   Cut deep diagonal slits in both sides
of the fish. Place lemon grass, ginger,
the halved green chilli, lime leaves and
coriander plants in cavity of fish.

2   Half fill a wok with hot water and
bring to the boil. Place fish on a wire
rack and place above water. Cover wok
and steam for 10-15 minutes or until
flesh flakes when tested with a fork.

3   To make sauce, place red and green
chillies, garlic, ginger, stock, lime juice
and fish sauce in a small saucepan, bring
to simmering over a low heat and simmer
for 4 minutes. To serve, place fish on a
serving plate and spoon over sauce.

*Serves 4*

Most Western kitchens
contain the equipment
required for Thai cooking.
At its most basic a wok or
large frying pan, several large
saucepans, a food processor
or a mortar and pestle and
possibly a multi-layered
steamer with a tight-fitting lid
are all that is needed.

# RICE & NOODLES

# PAD THAI

*Previous pages: Rice Noodles with Greens, Pad Thai*
*Opposite: Thai Fried Noodles*

315 g/10 oz fresh or dried rice noodles
2 teaspoons vegetable oil
4 red or golden shallots, chopped
3 fresh red chillies, chopped
2 tablespoons shredded fresh ginger
250 g/8 oz boneless chicken breast
fillets, chopped
250 g/8 oz medium uncooked prawns,
shelled and deveined
60 g/2 oz roasted peanuts, chopped
1 tablespoon sugar
4 tablespoons lime juice
3 tablespoons fish sauce
2 tablespoons light soy sauce
125 g/4 oz tofu, chopped
60 g/2 oz bean sprouts
4 tablespoons fresh coriander leaves
3 tablespoons fresh mint leaves
lime wedges to serve

In Thailand noodles are known as 'mee' and are frequently served as snacks.

1  Place noodles in a bowl and pour over boiling water to cover. If using fresh noodles soak for 2 minutes; if using dried noodles soak for 5-6 minutes or until soft. Drain well and set aside.

2  Heat oil in a frying pan or wok over a high heat, add shallots, chillies and ginger and stir-fry for 1 minute. Add chicken and prawns and stir-fry for 4 minutes or until cooked.

3  Add noodles, peanuts, sugar, lime juice and fish and soy sauces and stir-fry for 4 minutes or until heated through. Stir in tofu, bean sprouts, coriander and mint and cook for 1-2 minutes or until heated through. Serve with lime wedges.

*Serves 4*

# RICE NOODLES WITH GREENS

350 g/11 oz thick fresh or dried
rice noodles
1 tablespoon vegetable oil
2 tablespoons shredded fresh ginger
2 cloves garlic, crushed
250 g/8 oz Chinese broccoli
(gai lum), chopped
125 g/4 oz asparagus, cut in half
3 tablespoons snipped fresh garlic
chives
$^1$/3 cup/90 mL/3 fl oz stock
2 tablespoons light soy sauce
1 teaspoon cornflour blended with
2 teaspoons water

For more information about Chinese broccoli (gai lum) see hint on page 36.

1  Place noodles in a bowl and pour over boiling water to cover. If using fresh noodles soak for 2 minutes; if using dried noodles soak for 5-6 minutes or until soft. Drain well and set aside.

2  Heat oil in a wok or frying pan over a medium heat, add ginger and garlic and stir-fry for 1 minute. Add broccoli, asparagus, chives, stock and soy sauce and stir-fry for 2 minutes.

3  Add noodles to wok and stir-fry for 4 minutes or until heated through. Stir in cornflour mixture and cook for 1 minute or until mixture thickens.

*Serves 4*

# THAI FRIED NOODLES

vegetable oil for deep-frying
250 g/8 oz rice vermicelli noodles
2 teaspoons sesame oil
2 onions, chopped
2 cloves garlic, crushed
185 g/6 oz pork fillets, chopped
185 g/6 oz boneless chicken breast
fillets, chopped
1 teaspoon dried chilli flakes
125 g/4 oz bean sprouts
2 tablespoons Thai fish sauce (nam pla)
1 tablespoon lemon juice
2 teaspoons tamarind concentrate

1   Heat vegetable oil in a wok or large saucepan over a high heat until very hot. Deep-fry noodles, a few at a time, for 1-2 minutes or until lightly golden and puffed. Remove and set aside.

2   Heat sesame oil in a wok or frying pan over a meduim heat, add onions and garlic and stir-fry for 4 minutes or until soft and golden. Add pork, chicken and chilli flakes and stir-fry for 4 minutes or until pork and chicken are brown and cooked.

3   Add bean sprouts, fish sauce, lemon juice, tamarind and noodles and stir-fry for 2 minutes or until heated through. Serve immediately.

*Serves 4*

The success of this recipe lies in making sure that the oil is very hot before frying the noodles.

# THAI FRIED RICE

2 teaspoons vegetable oil
2 onions, chopped
4 rashers bacon, cut into strips
4 cloves garlic, thinly sliced
4 eggs, lightly beaten
2 cups/440 g/14 oz rice, cooked
3 tablespoons lime juice
2 tablespoons light soy sauce
1 tablespoon Thai fish sauce (nam pla)
3 plum (egg or Italian) tomatoes,
chopped
4 red or golden shallots, chopped
3 tablespoons fresh coriander leaves

1  Heat oil in a wok or frying pan over a medium heat, add onions, bacon and garlic and stir-fry for 4 minutes or until onions are golden. Remove and set aside.

2  Add eggs to wok, then swirl wok in a circular motion to coat with egg and cook for 1-2 minutes or until set. Remove omelette from pan, roll and cut into strips. Set aside.

3  Add rice, lime juice and soy and fish sauces to pan and stir-fry for 5 minutes or until heated through. Add tomatoes, shallots and coriander, then return onion mixture and omelette to pan and toss to combine.

*Serves 6*

Polished rice is usually eaten in Thailand – brown or untreated rice is considered to be inferior.

# STEAMED RICE IN BANANA LEAVES

2 cups/440 g/14 oz long grain white glutinous rice, soaked overnight
1 cup/250 mL/8 fl oz coconut cream
4 x 30 cm/12 in squares banana leaf or aluminium foil
220 g/7 oz boneless chicken breast fillet, sliced
4 red or golden shallots, chopped
3 fresh red chillies, chopped
2 tablespoons finely grated fresh ginger

2  Transfer rice to a bowl and fluff up with a fork. Stir in coconut cream and stand for 10 minutes.

3  Divide half the rice between the banana leaves or aluminium foil squares. Spread rice out evenly, then top with chicken, shallots, chillies and ginger. Cover with remaining rice and fold banana leaf or aluminium foil to enclose.

White glutinous rice can either be long or short grained and is sometimes called sweet or sticky rice. For savoury dishes such as this one, Thai cooks would use the long grain variety. Glutinous rice has a very high starch content, the cooked grains cling together in a mass and are soft and sticky. Short grain white glutinous rice is mainly used in sweets. You can also get a black glutinous rice, for more information about this rice see hint on page 74.

1  Drain rice, place in a colander and rinse under cold running water until water runs clear. Place rice in a saucepan and pour over enough water to just cover. Cover pan with a tight-fitting lid and cook over a medium-low heat for 20 minutes or until water is absorbed.

4  Half fill a wok with water and bring to the boil. Place parcels in a bamboo steamer. Place steamer on a wire rack in wok, cover steamer and steam for 10 minutes.

*Serves 4*

# CHILLI FRIED RICE

*Thai Fried Rice, Chilli Fried Rice, Steamed Rice in Banana Leaves*

2 teaspoons vegetable oil
2 fresh red chillies, chopped
1 tablespoon Thai red curry paste
2 onions, sliced
$1^1/_2$ cups/330 g/$10^1/_2$ oz rice, cooked
125 g/4 oz snake (yard-long) or
green beans, chopped
125 g/4 oz baby bok choy (Chinese
greens), blanched
3 tablespoons lime juice
2 teaspoons Thai fish sauce (nam pla)

1   Heat oil in a wok or frying pan over a high heat, add chillies and curry paste and stir-fry for 1 minute or until fragrant. Add onions and stir-fry for 3 minutes or until soft.

2   Add rice, beans and bok choy (Chinese greens) to pan and stir-fry for 4 minutes or until rice is heated through. Stir in lime juice and fish sauce.

*Serves 4*

This is a good way to turn leftover cooked rice into a tasty light meal.

# SWEETS

*Previous pages: Citrus Brûlée,*
*Tapioca Pudding with Figs*

# CITRUS BRULEE

1 3/4 cups/440 mL/14 fl oz pouring
cream (single)
3/4 cup/185 mL/6 fl oz coconut cream
3 thin strips orange rind, all white
pith removed
3 stalks fresh lemon grass, bruised,
each stalk cut into 3 pieces, or 3 thin
strips lemon rind, all white pith removed
6 egg yolks
1/3 cup/75 g/2 1/2 oz caster sugar
palm or brown sugar

1  Place cream, coconut cream, orange
rind and lemon grass or rind in a
saucepan and bring to the boil. Remove
from heat and set aside to cool slightly.

2  Place egg yolks and sugar in a bowl
and whisk until light and fluffy and

sugar dissolves. Whisk in half the
cream mixture, then whisk mixture
back into the remaining cream mixture.
Return pan to a low heat and cook,
stirring, until mixture thickens and
coats the back of a wooden spoon.

3  Strain mixture through a fine sieve
and divide between six 3/4 cup/185 mL/
6 fl oz capacity ramekins. Cool, then
cover and refrigerate for 12 hours or
until cold and very thick.

4  Sprinkle a little palm or brown sugar
over the surface of each brûlée and
cook under a preheated very hot grill
until sugar caramelises.

*Serves 6*

In step 2 it is important that
the mixture does not boil or it
will curdle.

# TAPIOCA PUDDING WITH FIGS

Oven temperature
160°C, 325°F, Gas 3

90 g/3 oz tapioca
1 tablespoon ground cardamom
2 pandan leaves, torn into pieces
1 1/2 cups/375 mL/12 fl oz coconut
cream
3/4 cup/185 g/6 oz palm or demerara
sugar
1/4 cup/60 mL/2 fl oz hot water
4 eggs, lightly beaten
3 tablespoons flaked coconut

CARAMELISED FIGS
4 fresh figs, halved
1/4 cup/60 g/2 oz palm or demerara
sugar

1  Place tapioca, cardamom, pandan
leaves and coconut cream in a saucepan
and bring to the boil. Reduce heat and
simmer for 5 minutes or until tapioca
swells slightly. Remove pan from heat
and stand for 5 minutes. Remove
pandan leaves.

2  Place palm or demerara sugar and
water in a bowl and mix to dissolve
sugar. Stir into tapioca mixture, then
add eggs and mix to combine.

3  Divide mixture evenly between six
lightly greased 1 cup/250 mL/8 fl oz
capacity timbale moulds or ramekins.
Sprinkle with flaked coconut. Place
moulds in a baking dish with enough
hot water to come halfway up the sides.
Bake for 45 minutes or until puddings
are firm. Stand for 10 minutes, then
turn out, keeping the top upper most.

4  For figs, sprinkle cut side of each fig
with a little palm or demerara sugar,
then cook under a preheated hot grill
for 3-5 minutes or until sugar caramelises
and figs are heated through. Serve with
puddings.

*Serves 6*

Pandan leaves are the
leaves of a small pandanus
palm or screwpine – there is
one of these palms in many
Thai gardens. The leaves are
used in both sweet and
savoury dishes and Thai
cooks usually add a strip to
rice when cooking it.
If figs are unavailable other
soft fresh fruit such as
apricots, peaches, mangoes
or nectarines can be used.

# CARDAMOM BANANA PUFFS

30 g/1 oz butter
1 teaspoon ground cardamom
2 small (about 315 g/10 oz) bananas,
sliced
1 tablespoon palm or brown sugar
2 teaspoons granulated coffee
dissolved in 2 teaspoons hot water
315 g/10 oz prepared puff pastry
vegetable oil for deep-frying
rose petals (optional)

BURNT ROSE WATER SYRUP
1 cup/250 g/8 oz sugar
1 cup/250 mL/8 fl oz water
1 tablespoon rose water

1   To make syrup, place sugar and
$^1/_2$ cup/125 mL/4 fl oz water in a
saucepan and cook, stirring, over a low
heat until sugar dissolves. Bring to the
boil, then cook over a medium heat
until syrup starts to turn brown.
Remove pan from heat, place in a sink,
then carefully stir in remaining water
and rose water. Return pan to heat and
cook, stirring, until caramel melts and is
smooth. Set aside to cool.

2   Melt butter in a frying pan over
a medium heat, add cardamom and
bananas and cook, stirring, for
1-2 minutes or until fragrant. Stir in
sugar and coffee mixture and mix to
coat bananas well. Cook for 3-4 minutes
longer or until mixture is thick. Remove
pan from heat and set aside to cool.

3   Roll out pastry to 3 mm/$^1/_8$ in thick
and using a 10 cm/4 in cutter, cut out
eight rounds. Place a spoonful of
banana mixture in the centre of each

pastry round. Brush edges lightly with
water and fold pastry over filling. Press
edges together, then pinch with your
thumb and index finger, fold pinched
edges over and pinch again.

4   Heat oil in a large saucepan until a
cube of bread dropped in browns in
50 seconds and cook 2 puffs at a time for
3-4 minutes or until puffed and golden.
Drain on absorbent kitchen paper. To
serve, drizzle with rose water syrup and
scatter with a few rose petals (if using).

*Makes 8*

Take care when adding the
extra water and the rose
water, as the syrup will 'spit'
profusely. For safety, place
the saucepan in the sink,
wear an oven mitt and
angle the saucepan away
from you. The syrup will
thicken considerably on
cooling.

*Cardamom Banana Puffs*

# STICKY RICE AND MANGO

2 cups/440 g/14 oz short grain white
glutinous rice, soaked overnight
1 cup/250 mL/8 fl oz coconut milk
3 tablespoons sugar
6 tablespoons very thick coconut cream
2 mangoes, peeled and sliced

This dish could also be made using black glutinous rice. Black glutinous rice is very popular in Thailand and is sometimes called black sticky rice. This rice still has the outer bran layer attached giving it its black colour. The inner grain is white but because black colour runs as the rice cooks the cooked rice is a black sticky mass.

1   Drain rice, place in a colander and rinse under cold running water until water runs clear.

2   Place rice in a saucepan and pour enough cold water to cover. Cover pan with a tight-fitting lid and and cook over a low heat for 15-20 minutes or until water evaporates.

3   Place rice in a shallow dish and stir with a fork. Combine coconut milk and sugar and stir into rice. Cover and stand for 25 minutes.

4   To serve, spoon rice into serving dishes, top with 1 tablespoon thick coconut cream and serve with mangoes.

*Serves 6*

# STEAMED COCONUT CUSTARDS

1/2 cup/125 g/4 oz sugar
1 1/4 cups/315 mL/10 fl oz coconut milk
4 eggs, lightly beaten
fresh lychees or fresh fruit
of your choice

1   Place sugar, coconut milk and eggs in a bowl and beat until well combined. Pour mixture through a fine sieve and divide evenly between six ³/4 cup/185 mL/ 6 fl oz capacity ramekins.

2   Half fill a wok with hot water and bring to the boil. Place ramekins in a bamboo steamer. Place on wire rack in wok, cover steamer and steam gently for 20-25 minutes or until custards are set. Serve with lychees or fresh fruit.

*Serves 6*

# COCONUT PANCAKES

2 cups/375 g/12 oz rice flour
1/2 cup/125 g/4 oz sugar
2 1/2 cups/600 mL/1 pt coconut milk
3 eggs, lightly beaten
1 cup/90 g/3 oz flaked coconut
palm or brown sugar
fresh lime juice
mango or banana slices

An easy way to transfer pancake batter from the bowl to the pan is to use a soup ladle.

1   Place flour, sugar, coconut milk and eggs in a bowl and whisk until smooth. Stir in coconut.

2   Pour a little mixture into a heated, lightly greased 18 cm/7 in crêpe pan and tilt pan so that batter covers base thinly and evenly. Cook for 1 minute or until golden, turn pancake and cook on second side for 30 seconds. Remove from pan, set aside and keep warm. Repeat with remaining batter. To serve, sprinkle with a little palm or brown sugar, drizzle with a little lime juice and accompany with mango or banana slices.

*Serves 6*

# EASY THAI DINNER FOR SIX

## Shopping List

### Meat, Poultry and Fish

- [ ] 250 g/8 oz boneless chicken breast fillets
- [ ] 4 boneless chicken breast fillets
- [ ] 250 g/8 oz lean topside or round steak
- [ ] 500 g/1 lb round or blade steak
- [ ] 250 g/8 oz lean pork fillets or steak
- [ ] 500 g/1 lb lean pork strips
- [ ] 750 g/1$^1$/$_2$ lb boneless firm white fish fillets
- [ ] 12 medium uncooked prawns
- [ ] 12 mussels

### Fruit and Vegetables

- [ ] banana leaves
- [ ] 1 bunch/500 g/1 lb baby bok choy (Chinese greens)
- [ ] 6 fresh red chillies
- [ ] 2 fresh green chillies
- [ ] 2 large bunches fresh basil
- [ ] 2 large bunches fresh coriander
- [ ] 1 large bunch fresh mint
- [ ] 2 heads garlic
- [ ] fresh ginger
- [ ] 1 bunch fresh lemon grass or 1 fresh lemon
- [ ] 4 fresh limes
- [ ] 14 kaffir lime leaves
- [ ] 125 g/4 oz assorted lettuce leaves
- [ ] 1 orange
- [ ] 125 g/4 oz oyster or straw mushrooms
- [ ] 155 g/5 oz pea eggplant (aubergines) or 1 large eggplant (aubergine)
- [ ] 10 red or golden shallots

### Supermarket items

- [ ] 220 g/7 oz canned bamboo shoots
- [ ] 1.2 litres/2 pt coconut milk
- [ ] 500 mL/16 fl oz coconut cream
- [ ] 500 mL/16 fl oz pouring cream (single)
- [ ] 90 g/3 oz roasted peanuts
- [ ] 2 litres/3$^1$/$_2$ pt chicken or vegetable stock

## Pantry Check

- [ ] black peppercorns
- [ ] caster sugar
- [ ] ground coriander
- [ ] 8 eggs
- [ ] jasmine rice
- [ ] palm or brown sugar
- [ ] shrimp paste
- [ ] soy sauce
- [ ] light soy sauce
- [ ] sugar
- [ ] Thai fish sauce (nam pla)
- [ ] Thai red curry paste
- [ ] vegetable oil

## Work Plan

### THE DAY BEFORE

- ◆ **Brûlée:** Make brûlées up to end of step 3.
- ◆ **Satay:** Make satay sauce. Store in refrigerator.

### 3 HOURS BEFORE SERVING

- ◆ **Satay:** Thread meat onto skewers. Place in a shallow glass or ceramic dish. Pour over marinade. Cover. Store in refrigerator.
- ◆ **Soup:** Prepare ingredients. Cover. Store in refrigerator.
- ◆ **Salad:** Cook chicken. Cool. Slice. Store in refrigerator. Arrange herbs and lettuce leaves on serving platter. Cover. Store in refrigerator. Make dressing.
- ◆ **Pork with Garlic and Pepper:** Prepare ingredients. Cover. Store in refrigerator.

## Menu

**Chicken, Beef and Pork Satay**
(use ¹/₂ recipe quantity of meat or chicken for each type of satay. Make full quantity of sauce) (page 8)

**Hot and Sour Seafood Soup**
(page 19)

**Chicken Salad with Basil**
(page 24)

**Pork with Garlic and Pepper**
(page 34)

**Red Beef Curry** (page 46)

**Steamed Fish Mousse**
(page 62)

**Steamed Jasmine Rice**

**Citrus Brûlée**
(page 72)

- ◆ **Curry:** Prepare ingredients. Cover. Store in refrigerator.
- ◆ **Mousse:** Make banana leaf cups. Store in refrigerator. Make mousse mixture as directed in step 2 of recipe. Set aside.

### 45-30 MINUTES BEFORE SERVING

- ◆ **Curry:** Start cooking.
- ◆ **Salad:** Complete preparation, but do not dress.
- ◆ **Satay Sauce:** Remove from refrigerator.
- ◆ **Brûlée:** Sprinkle with sugar. Grill.

### FINISHING UP

- ◆ **Satay:** Drain skewers. Cook. Reheat sauce.
- ◆ **Mousse:** Pour coconut mixture into banana cups. Steam.
- ◆ **Soup:** Make soup.
- ◆ **Rice:** Cook. Remember to serve steaming hot.
- ◆ **Salad:** Drizzle with dressing.
- ◆ **Pork with Garlic and Pepper:** Cook.

*Clockwise from top: Steamed Fish Mousse, steamed jasmine rice, Red Beef Curry, Pork with Garlic and Pepper, Chicken Salad with Basil*

# GLOSSARY

**BANANA LEAVES:** Before using fresh banana leaves for wrapping food they need to be softened. This can be done by: passing the leaves over a gas flame until they are soft; blanching in boiling water for 20-30 seconds; or heating in the microwave on HIGH (100%) for 45-60 seconds or until soft. Remove the thick mid-rib before using or the leaves will be difficult to wrap around the food.

**BASIL:** Thai cooks use three main types of basil in cooking: Asian sweet or cinnamon basil, known in Thailand as horapa, is usually added at the end of cooking to give a final aromatic fragrance to the food. Holy basil, known as kaprao, is used in strongly flavoured dishes and is cooked in the dishes to impart its flavour. Lemon basil, known as manglak, as the name suggests has a lemon scent. It is mainly used in soups and sprinkled over salads. Ordinary basil can be used in place of any of the above. In this book the recipes do not specify which type of basil to use, but for an authentic Thai flavour choose the appropriate basil as discussed above.

**BITTER MELON (GOURD):** This cucumber-like melon has a lumpy skin and as the name suggests has a bitter taste. To use, peel, remove seeds and cut into cubes, strips or thin slices, then degorge by sprinkling with salt and allowing to stand for about 1 hour. Rinse under cold water and drain well. The degorging reduces bitterness, but to further reduce bitterness the melon can also be blanched in boiling water for a few minutes.

**COCONUT MILK/CREAM:** Coconut milk and coconut cream are essentially the same product. Coconut cream is very thick coconut milk and is the result of the first pressing of the coconut flesh. Coconut milk can be purchased in a number of forms – canned, as a long-life product in cartons or as a powder to which your add water. Once opened, it has a short life and should be used within a day or so.

You can make coconut milk using desiccated coconut and water. To make coconut milk, place 500 g/1 lb desiccated coconut in a bowl and pour over 3 cups/750 mL/1$\frac{1}{4}$ pt boiling water. Leave to stand for 30 minutes, then strain, squeezing the coconut to extract as much liquid as possible. This will make a thick coconut milk or what is referred to in this book as coconut cream. The coconut can be used again to a make thinner coconut milk, the product referred to as coconut milk in this book.

**COCONUT VINEGAR:** Made from the sap of the coconut palm, coconut vinegar is available from Oriental food shops. If unavailable, any mild vinegar can be used.

**CORIANDER:** The leaves, seeds and roots of this plant are used in Thai cooking. It is considered to be essential to Thai cuisine and almost every dish is garnished with fresh coriander leaves. The three parts of the plant all have a distinctively different flavour and one should not be substituted for another.

**CURRY PASTES**
Curry pastes are readily available from supermarkets and Oriental food shops. Homemade curry pastes are easy to make and will keep for about a week if stored in an airtight container in the refrigerator.

**Thai Green Curry Paste:** Chop 6 spring onions, 8 fresh green chillies, 4 cloves garlic and 2 stalks fresh lemon grass. Heat 1 tablespoon vegetable oil in a frying pan over a medium heat. Add spring onions, chillies, lemon grass and garlic. Cook, stirring, for 3 minutes or until soft. Cool slightly. Place garlic mixture, 1 tablespoon finely grated lime rind, 2 teaspoons lime juice, 2 tablespoons chopped fresh coriander leaves, 1 tablespoon ground coriander, 2 teaspoons ground cumin, 1 teaspoon ground turmeric and 2 tablespoons brown sugar and 1 teaspoon shrimp paste (optional) in a food processor or blender. Process to make a smooth paste. Heat 2 tablespoons vegetable oil in a frying pan over a medium heat. Add paste. Cook, stirring constantly, for 5 minutes or until a thick paste forms.
Makes 1 cup/250 mL/8 fl oz

**Thai Red Curry Paste:** Chop 8 small fresh red chillies, 6 spring onions, 6 cloves garlic and 2 stalks fresh lemon grass. Heat 3 tablespoons vegetable oil in a frying pan over a medium heat. Add chillies, spring onions, garlic, lemon grass and 1 teaspoon caraway seeds. Cook, stirring, for 3 minutes or until golden. Cool slightly. Place onion mixture, 2 tablespoons ground coriander, 2 tablespoons finely grated fresh galangal (optional), 2 teaspoons Thai fish sauce (nam pla), 2 teaspoons lime juice, 2 teaspoons finely grated lime rind and 1 teaspoon shrimp paste in a food processor or blender. Shred 6 kaffir lime leaves. Add to processor. Process to make a smooth paste. Heat 2 tablespoons vegetable oil in a frying pan over a medium heat. Add paste. Cook, stirring, for 5 minutes or until a thick paste forms. Makes 1 cup/250 mL/8 fl oz

**DRIED SHRIMPS:** These can be purchased whole or shredded in plastic packets from Oriental food stores. If stored in the refrigerator they should last for several months. Choose shrimps which are a salmon pink colour and slightly soft – very hard shrimps or those that smell of ammonia should be avoided.

**GALANGAL:** This spice belongs to the same family as ginger. In Thai cooking it is usually greater galangal that is used. Where other Asian cuisines would use ginger, Thai cooks use galangal. It can be purchased fresh or bottled in brine. Bottled galangal is more tender and not as fibrous as the fresh product and as such is somewhat easier to use. Bottled galangal will keep for months in the refrigerator. If

unavailable fresh ginger can be used instead, but will give a different flavour to the finished dish.

**KAFFIR LIMES:** Both the fruit and the leaves of this citrus tree are used in Thai cooking. Both have a distinctive flavour and perfume. The leaves are available dried, fresh frozen or fresh from Oriental food shops and some greengrocers. If kaffir lime leaves are unavailable a little finely grated lime rind can be used instead. The fruit of the kaffir lime is very dark green with a thick, bumpy and wrinkled rind. In this book we have not specified the use of kaffir limes for lime juice, but for a true Thai flavour use it whenever possible.

**LEMON GRASS:** Fresh lemon grass is available from Oriental food shops and some supermarkets and greengrocers. It is also available dried: if using dried lemon grass, soak it in hot water for 20 minutes or until soft before using. Lemon grass can be purchased in bottles from supermarkets – use this in the same way as you would fresh lemon grass. There is also a powdered form available which is called sereh, this is strong in flavour and should be used with discretion. If lemon grass is unavailable, lemon balm, lemon verbena or lemon rind are possible substitutes.

**ORIENTAL RICE PAPER:** This is made from a paste of ground rice and water which is stamped into rounds and dried. When moistened the brittle sheets become flexible. It is used to make delicacies such as the Herbed Vegetable Rolls on page 8. Sold in sealed packets rice paper can be purchased from Oriental food stores. Oriental rice paper should not be confused with the fine, wafer-like rice paper used for confectionery.

**PALM SUGAR:** This is a rich, aromatic sugar extracted from the sap of various palms. The palm sugar used in Thailand is lighter and more refined than that used in other parts of Asia. Palm sugar is available from Oriental food shops.

**PEA EGGPLANT (AUBERGINE):** These tiny green eggplant (aubergines) are about the size of a green pea that are usually purchased still attached to the vine. They are used whole, can be eaten raw or cooked and have a bitter taste. If unavailable green peas can be used instead.

**RICE**
Rice is the central dish of any Thai meal and the other dishes are considered to be side dishes.
**Jasmine rice:** For an authentic Thai meal serve steamed jasmine rice – cooked without salt. Jasmine rice is also called Thai fragrant rice and as its name suggests is delicately scented.
**White glutinous rice:** This rice can either be long or short grained and is sometimes called sweet or sticky rice. For savoury dishes, Thai cooks would use the long grain variety. Glutinous rice is very high in starch content, the cooked grains cling together in a mass and are soft and sticky. Short grain white glutinous rice is mainly used for desserts.

**SHALLOTS:** The shallots used in this book are a small golden, purple or red onion. They are 2.5-5 cm/ 1-2 in long and have a more intense flavour than large onions. The golden shallots are sweeter than the red or purple ones. The shallots used in Asian cooking are similar to the French échalote, which may be used if the Asian-style are unavailable. Thinly sliced raw shallots make a good salad garnish or they can be slowly deep-fried until crisp and golden for an exotic garnish.

**SHRIMP PASTE:** This pungent ingredient is available from Oriental food shops and some supermarkets. It is made by pounding dried salted shrimp to a paste. Do not be put off by the odour of this paste as this disappears when cooked with other ingredients. Available both fresh or dried. If using dried shrimp paste in place of fresh, use only about half as much. Anchovy paste can be used instead if shrimp paste is unavailable; use about half the quantity that you would with dried shrimp paste. In this book, fresh shrimp paste is used.

**SNAKE (YARD-LONG) BEANS:** As their name suggests these are very long thin green beans. They are known by a variety of names including asparagus bean, pea bean, cow pea and China pea and it is the dried seeds of this bean which become black-eyed peas. If unavailable ordinary green beans can be used.

**TAMARIND:** This is the large pod of the tamarind or Indian date tree. After picking, it is seeded and peeled then pressed into a dark brown pulp. To use, soak the pulp in water, then strain and use as directed in the recipe. The usual dilution is three parts water to one part tamarind. There is also a tamarind concentrate available, if using this it should be diluted with double the amount of water that you would use when diluting the pulp. Tamarind is available from Indian food shops. If unavailable, use a mixutre of lime or lemon juice and treacle as a substitute.

# INDEX

Banana Cardamom Puffs   73
Barbecued Pork Spare Ribs   61
Barbecued Squid Salad   28
Beef
    and Bean Stir-fry   37
    Cashew and Chilli, Curry   46
    Curry Puffs   14
    Red, Curry   46
    Satay   8
    Spiced Grilled   60
    Thai, Salad   26
    with Peppercorns   32
Bitter Melon, Stir-fried   38
Burnt Rose Water Syrup   73

Caramelised Figs   72
Cardamom
    and Orange Duck   44
    Banana Puffs   73
Cashew and Chilli Beef Curry   46
Cellophane Noodle Salad   27
Charcoal-grilled Chicken   58
Chicken
    and Coconut Soup   18
    Charcoal-grilled   58
    Pad Thai   66
    Phanaeng Curry   52
    Rose Petal Salad   25
    Salad with Basil   24
    Satay   8
    Steamed Rice in Banana Leaves   68
    Thai Fried Noodles   67
    Thai Green, Curry   44
    with Chilli Jam   32
    with Garlic and Pepper   58
    with Lime and Coconut   52
Chilli
    and Prawn Curry   50
    and Tamarind Dressing   12
    Deep-fried Fish   56
    Fried Rice   69
    Jam   32
    Kumara Soup   20
    Red Sauce   56
    Sweet, Sauce   10
Citrus Brûlée   72
Coconut
    and Chicken Soup   18
    Chicken with Lime and   52
    Pancakes   74
    Prawns and Scallops   33
    Steamed Custards   74

Crab and Pork Balls   10
Crispy Noodles with Lime Pickle   9
Cucumber Relish   13
Curry
    Beef Puffs   14
    Cardamom and Orange Duck   44
    Cashew and Chilli Beef   46
    Chicken Phanaeng   52
    Chicken with Lime and
        Coconut   52
    Green Chilli and Prawn   50
    Green Mango and Fish   50
    Minted Bean   45
    Pork and Pineapple with Basil   49
    Red Beef   46
    Sweet Potato and Tofu   48
    Thai Green Chicken   44

Deep-fried Chilli Fish   56
Desserts
    Cardamom Banana Puffs   73
    Citrus Brûlée   72
    Coconut Pancakes   74
    Steamed Coconut Custards   74
    Sticky Rice and Mango   74
    Tapioca Pudding with Figs   72
Dressing
    Chilli and Basil   24
    Chilli and Lime   24
    Lemon and Chilli   28
    Lime   25
    Lime and Coconut   28
    Lime and Coriander   26
    Tamarind and Chilli   12
Duck
    Cardamom and Orange   44
    Stir-fried, with Greens   36

Eggplant and Basil Stir-fry   38

Filling
    Crab and Pork   10
    Herbed Vegetable   8
    Pork and Coriander   14
    Spicy Beef   14
Fish
    and Green Mango Curry   50
    Cakes with Relish   13
    Deep-fried Chilli   56
    Hot and Sour Seafood Soup   19
    Steamed Mousse   62
    with Green Mango Sauce   56
    with Lime and Garlic   62

Green Chilli and Prawn Curry   50
Green Mango

and Fish Curry   50
Salad   24
Sauce with Fish   56

Herbed Vegetable Rolls   8
Hot and Sour
    Prawn Soup   18
    Seafood Soup   19

Lime
    and Garlic Sauce   62
    and Garlic with Fish   62
    Chicken with, and Coconut   52
    Crab Topping   11
    Crab, with Rice Cakes   11
    Pickle   9

Mango
    and Sticky Rice   74
    Green, and Fish Curry   50
    Green, Salad   24
Minted Bean Curry   45
Mussels
    Hot and Sour Seafood Soup   19
    with Coconut Vinegar   41
    with Lemon Grass   57
    with Tamarind   12

Noodles
    Cellophane, Salad   27
    Crispy, with Lime Pickle   9
    Pad Thai   66
    Rice, with Greens   66
    Thai Fried   67

Orange and Cardamom Duck   44

Pad Thai   66
Pancakes, Coconut   74
Pork
    and Crab Balls   10
    and Pineapple with Basil   49
    and Pumpkin Stir-fry   34
    Barbecued Spare Ribs   61
    Rose Petal Salad   25
    Satay   8
    Spring Rolls   14
    Thai Fried Noodles   67
    with Garlic and Pepper   34
Prawn/s
    and Green Chilli Curry   50
    and Pawpaw Salad   28
    Coconut, and Scallops   33
    Hot and Sour Seafood Soup   19
    Hot and Sour Soup   18
    Pad Thai   66

Rose Petal Salad    25
Stir-fried Tamarind    40
Pumpkin
    and Pork Stir-fry    34

Red Chilli Sauce    56
Rice
    Cakes with Lime Crab    11
    Chilli Fried    69
    Noodles with Greens    66
    Steamed in Banana Leaves    68
    Sticky, and Mango    74
    Thai Fried    68
Rolls
    Herbed Vegetable    8
    Pork Spring    14
Rose Petal Salad    25

Salad
    Barbecued Squid    28
    Cellophane Noodle    27
    Chicken, with Basil    24
    Green Mango    24
    Prawn and Pawpaw    28
    Rose Petal    25
    Thai Beef    26
Satay
    Beef    8
    Chicken    8
    Pork    8

Sauce
    Green Mango    56
    Lime and Garlic    62
    Red Chilli    56
    Satay    8
    Sweet Chilli    10
Scallops
    with Lemon Grass    57
Seafood
    Hot and Sour Soup    19
    Shellfish with Lemon Grass    57
Shellfish
    Coconut Prawns and Scallops    33
    Hot and Sour Prawn Soup    18
    Hot and Sour Seafood Soup    19
    with Lemon Grass    57
Soup
    Chicken and Coconut    18
    Chilli Kumara    20
    Hot and Sour Prawn    18
    Hot and Sour Seafood    19
    Thai Vegetable    20
Spiced Grilled Beef    60
Squid
    Barbecued, Salad    28
Steamed
    Coconut Custards    74
    Crab and Pork Balls    10
    Fish Mousse    62
    Rice in Banana Leaves    68

Sticky Rice and Mango    74
Stir-fry
    Beef and Bean    37
    Beef with Peppercorns    32
    Bitter Melon    38
    Chicken with Chilli Jam    32
    Coconut Prawns and Scallops    33
    Duck with Greens    36
    Eggplant and Basil    38
    Mussels with Coconut Vinegar    41
    Pork and Pumpkin    34
    Pork with Garlic and Pepper    34
    Tamarind Prawns    40
Sweet Potato and Tofu Curry    48

Tapioca Pudding with Figs    72
Thai
    Beef Salad    26
    Fried Noodles    67
    Fried Rice    68
    Green Chicken Curry    44
    Vegetable Soup    20
Tofu
    and Sweet Potato Curry    48
    Thai Vegetable Soup    20

Vegetable
    Herbed Rolls    8
    Thai Soup    20